GETTING IN

A Step-by-Step Plan for Gaining Admission to Graduate School in Psychology

American Psychological Association, Washington, DC

Seventh printing March 2002

Published by the
American Psychological Association
750 First Street, NE
Washington, DC 20002

Copies may be ordered from
APA Order Department
P.O. Box 92984
Washington, DC 20090-2984

In the UK and Europe, copies may be ordered from
American Psychological Association
3 Henrietta Street
Covent Garden, London
WC2E 8LU England

This book was typeset in Futura and New Baskerville by Easton Publishing Services, Inc., Easton, MD

Printer: Data Reproductions Corp., Auburn Hills, MI
Cover illustrator: Joe VanDerBos, San Francisco, CA
Cover designer: Anne Masters, Washington, DC
Technical/production editor: Olin J. Nettles

Library of Congress Cataloging-in-Publication Data
Getting in : a step-by-step for gaining admission to graduate school in psychology /
    American Psychological Association.
        p.   cm.
    Includes index.
    ISBN 1-55798-219-8 (acid-free paper)
    1. Psychology—Study and teaching (Graduate)—United States.   2. Universities
and colleges—Graduate work.   3. Universities and colleges—Admission.
    I. American Psychological Association.
    BF80.7.U6G47 1993
    150'.71'173—dc20   93-33069
                                                                            CIP

British Library Cataloguing-in-Publication Data
A CIP record is available from the British Library.

Printed in the United States of America

Contents

Preface

Each year, thousands of promising individuals apply to graduate school in psychology, but only a small percentage get in. Others are discouraged from even applying when they see common applicant-to-opening ratios of 25-to-1 or higher. Many of these rejected and would-be applicants could have made excellent psychologists. What they lacked was not academic ability or career potential, but insider knowledge of the application process and a rational strategy for applying that works. It was for this reason that *Getting In* was written.

We believed that graduate applicants would benefit from a book that helped them maximize their chances of success while minimizing needless anxiety. We also thought that undergraduate advisors would find such a book to be a useful supplement to their face-to-face meetings with students. We hope that applicants and advisors alike will benefit from the step-by-step plan we have provided.

This book is about beating the odds of getting into graduate school by selecting the right programs to apply to (those that are the best match) and showcasing both abilities and potential in just the right way (and at every step). It is about making informed choices. It is about doing one's best. If you are even thinking about applying to graduate school in psychology or are providing guidance to someone who is, *Getting In* is for you.

Many individuals shared their insights and expertise with us to make this book a reality. We are deeply indebted to Cynthia Baum, PhD, and to Jessica Kohout, PhD, for their incisive suggestions and constructive comments on various drafts of the manuscript. Peter Petrossian worked tirelessly to obtain current information from various APA offices and directorates; we are grateful for his diligent efforts on our behalf. Gwendolyn Keita, PhD, helped us to network with faculty who could speak to the needs of several specific populations. We are particularly thankful for discerning observations and contributions from APA staff members Clinton Anderson, Brendan Cooney, Jeannie Coscia, Albert Figueroa, Ernesto Guerra, Sandy Hauck, Jeanie Kelleher, Jill Mathis, Todd Mook, Sonja Preston, Ismael Rivera, and Marlene Wicherski.

Conversations with faculty, university administrators, financial aid directors, and graduate students expanded our understanding of many facets of the application process and of graduate student life. The faculty and administrative perspective on applying to graduate school was graciously shared by John Allen, PhD, Robin Buhrke, PhD, Harold Cook, PhD, Richard Cox, PhD, Lucia Albino Gilbert, PhD, Paul Issac, PhD, Mary Beth Kenkel, PhD, Bernice Lott, PhD, Patricia Morokoff, PhD, Richard O'Brien, PhD, and George Spivack, PhD. Christine Browning, PhD, at the Counseling Center of the University of California, Irvine, and Sandra Feldman, PhD, who is in private practice, also shared their expertise about applicants who are members of specific populations. Rhona Hartman from the HEATH (Higher Education and Adult Training for People With Handicaps) Resource Center and Jane Jarrow, PhD, from AHSSPPE (Association on Handicapped Student Service Programs in Postsecondary Education), together with Lynne Bond, PhD, and Ralph Swenson, JD, from the University of Vermont, provided invaluable advice about concerns of students with disabilities. Critical tips on the logistics of applying for financial aid were provided by Vicki Baker, Jennifer Douglas, Stephanie Greenstein, Alice Oliver, Robin Robinson, and Anne Sturtevant, all directors of financial aid at universities across the country. Likewise, we are grateful to graduate students James Cantor, Karen Jordan, Elizabeth Leonard, Jennifer Pastor, Marie Billye Simmers, Robin Soler, Sylvie Taylor, Mun Wong, and Miguel Ybarra for making us aware of many important student concerns.

Finally, we are grateful for the creative contributions of Mary Lynn Skutley, Deanna D'Errico, and Peggy Schlegel, who acted as advocates to help craft a book that would be maximally accessible to all readers. We are also indebted to Judy Nemes for editorial suggestions and research support and to Olin Nettles for skillful copyediting and production.

We are interested in keeping future versions of this book up-to-date and pertinent to contemporary graduate school applicants. If you have any comments or suggestions, please contact the Director of Acquisitions and Development, APA Books, 750 First Street, NE, Washington, DC 20002-4242. Your feedback will be welcome.

Why and How You Should Use This Book

If we really want to live, we'd better start at once to try.

—*W. H. Auden*

Congratulations! If you have decided to read this book, you have already begun to conquer one of the major obstacles to getting into graduate school and on with your life: anxiety. Most potential applicants feel overwhelmed when they begin to seriously consider graduate school. As a result, some procrastinate and others act impulsively, neither of which is likely to result in success. By picking up this book, you have chosen a different path: to tolerate and manage your anxiety while you plan a reasonable application strategy with a high probability of success.

Fortunately, planning is one of the most adaptive ways of managing your anxiety. We have designed this book to help you plan in the most effective and efficient way that we know. First, we have broken down the process into manageable steps and substeps. Second, we have included handy worksheets and checklists that you can photocopy or modify to streamline the application process. Finally, we have kept the length of this book to a minimum, while covering all of the most important bases.

This book is written specifically for people who are either considering or definitely planning to apply to graduate psychology programs—several years from now, or perhaps as soon as next year. For those of you who are uncertain, don't feel that you have to make a full commitment to go to graduate school in order to use this book. You need only commit to a first step: learning about the process of deciding. When you have completed that step, you will have information that you don't have now that might lead you to take a second step, such as researching programs, or to take a different path altogether. In either case, you will have given yourself the opportunity to explore and learn about your options.

One major audience for this book consists of those who are working on or have recently completed an undergraduate degree in psychology. But the information in this book applies to potential applicants who may fit other descriptions as well, including the many individuals who are returning to school later in life, students who are currently enrolled in master's programs or are recipients of master's degrees in psychology, nonpsychology majors, nonpsychology degree holders, foreign-born students, and psychology doctorates seeking to respecialize. We have included information that may be particularly useful to specific populations of applicants, such as ethnic minority students; women; gay, lesbian, and bisexual individuals; and students with disabilities.

This book can also be used by faculty advisors and college counseling staff, who field thousands of questions about admission to graduate study in psychology each year. We hope this book will be useful to these advisors and counselors, both as a resource for students and as a source of useful ideas to help students plan their academic careers.

Why Read This Book?

We don't want to scare you away with discouraging statistics. Yes, the competition for available openings in graduate school in psychology is fierce, and, yes, the admission standards are high.[1] The application process can be daunting and will require you to invest considerable time and money. You will have to be disciplined, organized, and tenacious to succeed. Furthermore, even after you've met that challenge and are accepted, you will be expected to devote considerably more time, money, and effort to earn your degree. In view of these investments, you'll want to be sure that the potential returns are worth it and that you have what it takes to succeed. If they are and you do, we think this book can help you become the best possible candidate you can be.

We encourage you to read this book from cover to cover and to be actively involved in working through the steps we outline (have notepaper, pencils, and a calendar in hand). You may judge yourself to have strong credentials and to be ready to fill out an application right now. However, not having been through this process before, you may be unaware of some crucial information that could seriously affect your chances of ac-

---

1. The programs receiving the most applications are accredited programs in clinical psychology offering the PhD. Using a random sample of 50 such programs listed in *Graduate Study in Psychology*, we calculated that the applicant-to-opening ratio went from a low of 3 to 1 to a high of 65 to 1, with the majority of programs having ratios between 11 to 1 and 40 to 1. Other programs are less competitive but still have high standards for admission, as you will see when you read chapters 2 and 4 and look at specific program entries in *Grad Study*.

ceptance. Following the advice in this book could make the difference between getting into your first-choice schools or having to settle for something less.

How This Book Is Organized

You will complete five major steps in applying to graduate school. You will

1. decide whether graduate school in psychology is right for you.
2. define the area of concentration and degree that you will pursue.
3. choose a range of programs to apply to.
4. complete applications to these programs.
5. attend interviews (possibly) and make a final decision regarding which program you will attend.

Step 1 is covered in chapters 2 and 4. Chapter 2, "Is a Graduate Degree in Psychology the Right Choice for You?," encourages you to examine your reasons for pursuing a graduate degree and to think about the day-to-day academic and practical realities of applying to and attending graduate school. Chapter 4, "Assessing Your Qualifications and Improving Your Chances for Acceptance," describes in more detail the variety of criteria used by selection committees to evaluate applicants. It also offers specific advice for assessing and improving your qualifications.

Step 2 is covered in chapter 3, "Decisions to Make Before Researching Graduate Programs in Psychology." This chapter helps you to further identify settings, populations, and work activities that would be a good match for you and to choose an appropriate training model, area of concentration, and degree to pursue. It lays the groundwork for zeroing in on those programs that offer exactly what you are looking for.

Step 3 is covered in chapter 5, "Choosing Which Programs to Apply To." Here you will narrow your options and target programs that are strong bets, good bets, and long shots, with an emphasis on the first two. Worksheets are provided to streamline the research and evaluation process. When you finish that chapter, you will be ready to begin filling out your applications.

Step 4 is covered in chapter 6, "Applying to Graduate Programs." We outline a sequence of eight steps you should take in preparing your applications, and we offer guidelines for when and how to negotiate each step. Scrupulous attention to every detail of these steps will considerably enhance your chances of success.

Step 5 is covered in chapter 7, "After You've Applied." In that chapter, we describe how to conduct yourself during preselection interviews, how to accept and decline offers, and what to do if you are not accepted by any of the programs to which you have applied.

Because each chapter builds on the one before it, it is important for you to read the whole book sequentially. In each of these chapters, you will find information about specific populations integrated into the general guidance offered. Following the text are several useful appendixes, which we will direct your attention to in specific places in the book. Finally, we have provided a resource list, which includes contact information for organizations mentioned in the book and a bibliography of publications you can consult for further information about many of the topics we discuss. The major resource you should plan to have on hand as you work through the steps outlined in this book is *Graduate Study in Psychology*, published by the American Psychological Association (APA) and updated each year. We will refer to this as *Grad Study* throughout the book. It is available for purchase through the APA and can also be found in most university libraries. International students may find it helpful to have other resources at hand, such as *Graduate Study in the United States: A Guide for Prospective International Graduate Students* (see Resources for this and other relevant publications).

When To Begin

It is never too early to begin planning your application strategy. The earlier you begin, the more opportunity you will have to maximize your effectiveness at each step along the way. Students who start to think about graduate school early in their junior year in college[2] can beef up their applications by selecting the most valued electives and by getting research or human service experience. They may also choose to join Psi Chi or Psi Beta (the national honor societies in psychology) and to attend state, regional, or national psychology conventions and learn firsthand about various programs' faculty. They will have ample time to study for the admissions

2. For potential applicants who have been out of school for a while, translate these time frames into months or years (e.g., September in the junior year would mean approximately 2 years before you plan to attend).

tests, such as the Graduate Record Examinations (GREs) and the Miller Analogies Test (MAT).

However, successful applications can still be planned as late as September of your senior year. This more "typical" timetable precludes some of the options described above and does require that you work more quickly and efficiently. If you begin in September of your senior year, you will need to set aside large chunks of your free time for the process, but you should have enough time to succeed.

We do *not* recommend that you begin any later than September of your senior year. For one thing, many programs have application deadlines of January 1, and October is the last date you can take the Psychology GRE and the paper-and-pencil version of the general GRE and still have scores reported by that time.[3] It takes time to line up the best professors to write your letters of recommendation, and to create application essays that will best represent you. If you start later than September, you may jeopardize these or other steps in the process. If you are reading this later in your senior year, it may pay to postpone your entrance into graduate school for one year and to take advantage of the extra time to enhance your qualifications (see chapters 4 and 7) and to apply in a careful, more methodical way. Although waiting may at first seem like a sacrifice, it may later prove to be a blessing.

Having said all of this, we do want you to know that there are students who have started quite late (e.g., over the Thanksgiving break of their senior year) and have still gotten accepted into the programs of their choice. If for some reason you are in this situation and *cannot* wait another year, read this book with an awareness that you will have to work on many steps in the process concurrently rather than sequentially. Pay particular attention to deadlines that are nonnegotiable (e.g., applying to take the Psychology GRE, allowing your professors a reasonable amount of time for writing your letters of recommendation).

In Exhibit 1.1 you will find a "typical" timetable that begins in

---

3. As this book was going to press, the Educational Testing Service (ETS) announced a cooperative agreement with the Sylvan Learning Centers to offer a computerized version of the general GRE (but not the Psychology GRE) at least three times each week at sites throughout the country (see Resources). By paying a higher fee, you can actually apply for and take the general GRE in the same week, on a space-available basis. You receive your results immediately, and they will be sent to graduate programs in approximately two to three weeks. The ETS has also indicated that they will phase out the pencil-and-paper version of the general GRE by 1997.

Exhibit 1.1

The "Typical" Timetable

SEPTEMBER

_____ Apply in the first week of September (or earlier) to take the GREs in October and to take the next scheduled MAT. Begin studying for them on a regular basis, and take practice exams to estimate what your score may be.

_____ Read chapters 2 through 5 of this book.

_____ Photocopy or modify the worksheet summarizing your qualifications and requirements.

_____ Find out what programs exist by carefully studying *Graduate Study in Psychology* and related catalogs.

_____ Compile a preliminary list of programs that offer the area of concentration, degree, and training you seek.

_____ Using the worksheets provided in chapter 5, compare your qualifications with admission requirements.

_____ Contact those programs that seem a good match to obtain additional information about the program and about financial aid. Ask for an application packet. Study this information carefully.

_____ Submit a request for your undergraduate transcript, which you will include in your packet for those who will eventually write letters of recommendation.

OCTOBER

_____ Using the strategy outlined and worksheets provided in chapter 5, compile a final list of programs that you will apply to. If you can afford it and it seems worthwhile, visit the campuses of programs that interest you most or that raise the most questions for you.

_____ Call the financial aid offices of all of the schools you will be applying to. Ask for an information packet about the aid available to graduate students, as well as any forms you will need to complete to be considered for financial aid.

_____ Take the GREs and the MAT; request scores to be sent to all of the schools you will apply to.

_____ Read chapter 6 of this book. Plan and schedule your application strategy. Pay careful attention to application deadlines, particularly with regard to financial aid, which often has *earlier* deadlines than the admissions application.

_____ Record goals for each week that remains before your applications must be submitted.

_____ Calculate application fees and make sure you have enough money to cover them (some schools waive this fee because of financial hardship; this needs to be checked with each school).

_____ Begin planning how you will obtain the money for any preselection interviews you may be required to attend.

_____ Begin contacting professors, other psychologists, and other individuals from whom you might want to request letters of recommendation.

continued

Exhibit 1.1, continued

NOVEMBER

_____ Request that your undergraduate transcript(s) be sent to all of the institutions you are applying to. Make sure your transcripts will be sent by your earliest application deadline.

_____ Prepare a resume to be used in your packet for those who will write your letters of recommendation.

_____ Finalize your decision regarding which professors to ask to write letters of recommendation, and recontact them to request letters.

_____ Begin thinking about the various essay questions each school requires. Allow time for your ideas to germinate. Write first drafts of essays.

_____ Begin filling out your financial aid and application forms.

_____ Supply individuals who will write your letters of recommendation with the packet you prepared earlier (see chapter 6).

DECEMBER

_____ Get feedback and write the final drafts of essays.

_____ Finalize financial aid forms.

_____ Finalize application forms.

_____ Carefully prepare _each_ application for mailing. Be sure to photocopy each in its entirety. Consider registered mail if you can afford it.

JANUARY/FEBRUARY

_____ Read chapter 7.

_____ Begin to prepare for possible preselection interviews (see chapter 7).

_____ Contact professors whom you have asked to submit letters of recommendation. Confirm that they were sent and thank those who sent them.

_____ Follow up to confirm that your applications are complete.

_____ Attend any preselection interviews you are invited to.

MARCH

_____ Follow the procedures outlined in chapter 7 for accepting and declining offers.

_____ If you are not accepted at any of the schools of your choice, consider the options outlined in chapter 7.

APRIL

_____ Finalize your financial arrangements for attending graduate school.

_____ Call or write the people who wrote your letters of recommendation and inform them of the outcome.

_____ Celebrate (or regroup).

Adapted from _Preparing for Graduate Study in Psychology: Not for Seniors Only!_ (pp. 32–33) by B. R. Fretz and D. J. Stang, 1980, Washington, DC: American Psychological Association.

September of the year before you plan to attend. In Appendix A, we have provided a timetable for early planners that begins in your junior year in college.[4] Both timetables are geared toward applicants applying to a doctoral program. If you decide to apply to a master's program, you may have a little more leeway because deadlines for applying to master's programs are often slightly later than those for doctoral programs, but this may vary from school to school. If you are applying to master's programs with later deadlines, you can adjust some parts of the timetable accordingly.

Reading this book during the summer before your senior year will allow you a little more time to spend on each step in the typical plan, and you may be able to include some steps from the timetable for early planners that is presented in Appendix A. If you are starting after September, you need to begin immediately with those steps that involve outside agents (e.g., test scores, transcripts, and letters of recommendation) and then play catch-up with the rest. Be sure, however, to read the sections pertaining to these steps (see the Table of Contents and the Index) and to follow advice as closely as you can, given your time constraints.

You may want to use these timetables as checklists to ensure that you have completed every task at a particular point in time. Applying to graduate school is a many-faceted process; it is easy to miss a step or two along the way.

Conclusion

If you were industrious enough to seek out a resource such as this, you are likely to be enterprising enough to succeed in gaining admission to graduate school in psychology. Many students bumble their way haphazardly through the application process without a plan. Some of these applicants are rejected not because they are not capable of graduate work, but because they shortchanged the application process. By reading this book, you will create a plan that you can pursue confidently from the first step until the last, a plan that can optimize your chances of success.

Pursuing a career in psychology as your lifework can be one of the

---

4. Both of these timetables were adapted from *Preparing for Graduate School in Psychology: Not for Seniors Only!* (pp. 32–33) by B. R. Fretz and D. J. Stang, 1980, Washington, DC: American Psychological Association.

most exciting and rewarding choices you'll ever make. For many of you, it can be a career that you never grow tired of and one that allows you flexibility in both roles and focus as you change and grow throughout your professional life. If you even *think* you might want to go to graduate school in psychology, take the next step by reading chapter 2. You owe it to yourself to "start at once to try."

2

Is a Graduate Degree in Psychology the Right Choice for You?

There is only one success—to be able to spend your life your own way.—*Christopher Morley*

Most of the major decisions that we make in life are made with partial information. If we waited to have *all* of the information we needed to predict an outcome, we'd probably never act. So you probably won't be able to know *everything* that would be useful to know in deciding whether to go to graduate school in psychology. But you can know *some* things that will increase your probability of making a choice that's right for you. What this and the next two chapters can do is help you glean the most information you can about yourself in terms of motivation, interests, skills, and qualifications, and about graduate education in terms of degrees, areas of concentration, and models of training. These chapters will also help you look at some of the practical realities of graduate school and decide whether that is the way you want to spend the next several years of your life.

In this chapter, to help you begin to answer the ultimate question of whether you should apply to graduate school, we guide you through four specific steps. These steps will encourage you to examine (a) your reasons for considering graduate study, (b) your academic suitability, (c) your personal suitability, and (d) the practical (e.g., time and money) implications of your decision.

Step 2.1: Define Your Reasons for Pursuing a Graduate Degree

There are a number of legitimate reasons for going to graduate school. Career preparation or advancement is one of the major reasons people pursue a graduate degree, and there are a wide range of career opportunities in psychology for which an advanced degree is necessary. For example, to teach at the college level, lead major research in a university or business setting, or practice clinical psychology without supervision, a doctoral degree is essential. To be competitive for many jobs in government and industry, a master's degree is increasingly required, and for many of these jobs a master's degree in psychology is ideal. The desire to gain employment in a field that requires an advanced degree in psychology is a highly appropriate reason for considering graduate school.

Other common reasons for pursuing a graduate degree in psychology are a deep and abiding interest in the discipline, an aspiration to contribute to a specific area of psychology, a love of learning, a desire for prestige and financial rewards, and a strong wish to improve the quality of life for individuals and for society. These reasons are more general than the career motives described above, so you will need to take some time to define how these goals might fit into a career plan that would require a graduate degree in psychology. What kind of psychologist would you need to be, for example, to contribute to an understanding of gender roles and adult achievement? Are you interested in generating basic knowledge in this area, or are you keen on applying such knowledge to work with individuals and groups? (We will talk more about this in chapter 3.)

What are *your* reasons for considering graduate study in psychology? Exactly what kind of work would you like to be doing several years from now? Is a graduate degree in psychology the best way to achieve your career goals, or are there other kinds of training that would enable you to realize those goals equally well? Are your aspirations well-focused, or is it possible that you really do not know what you want to do? We urge you to be honest with yourself (even if it's uncomfortable). If you are unclear about this and you admit it, you've taken the first step to becoming more focused. Now you can lay a plan to explore potential areas of interest and eventually become more sure of what you would like to do. Take time to remember what excited you about psychology in the first place. What areas did you pursue reading about? What topics in psychology classes excited you the most? What roles did you fantasize fulfilling?

Once you've answered these questions, begin to explore those areas in more detail. Scan journals that publish research and applications in those areas. (You will find a listing of such journals in *Journals in Psychology*; see Resources. Although the descriptions of journals in this publication are written for authors, they will also give you a good idea of what areas particular journals cover.) If you are still in school, talk to your undergraduate professors who work in those areas. Finally, chapter 3 of this book describes some of the settings in which psychologists work and activities in which they typically engage in a variety of areas. Reading that chapter carefully can also help you to decide which areas of psychology you are most interested in.

Making such an honest self-appraisal of your aspirations is the first step you should take toward answering the question "Is advanced study in psychology the right choice for me?" Indeed, psychology professors characterize their most successful students as being highly motivated (e.g., they have well-articulated goals) and having a marked passion for psychology. Strong aspirations will contribute both to being accepted in the program of your choice and to succeeding once you are in graduate school.

Step 2.2: Determine Whether You Have the Skills Necessary to Meet the Academic Demands of Graduate School in Psychology

Although we will outline the six most common skills necessary for success, no one can predict *exactly* what demands a particular program will make on you or the exact life-style you will be leading as a graduate student. Each program has its own "personality" that will call on different skills and learning styles of students. After you read this chapter, we encourage you to talk to graduate students and recent graduates in master's and doctoral programs, particularly in psychology. (Later in the process, we will suggest that you speak with graduate students at the programs to which you are most interested in applying.)

Ask a lot of questions. What is a typical day or week like? How many hours do they spend in class? Reading? Studying for exams? Writing papers? Making presentations? Working in a practicum? Doing research? What are their major stressors? How do they cope? What makes them want to quit? What makes it worth it to stay?

Try to picture yourself leading the kind of existence they describe. Learning as much as you can about academic life is especially relevant when you know that in substantial ways your life as a student will be quite similar to your life as an employed graduate. From day one of your program, you will be expected to think and act like the psychologist you will be when you graduate. As a graduate student, you will read widely; as an employed graduate, continuing to read scholarly books and journals throughout your career will be essential to keeping abreast of new developments in your field. Writing and public speaking, prominent features of your academic life, will remain so in your professional life because you will be expected to share the insights you gain in your particular line of work with the psychological community and the public. As a graduate, you will continue to be a consumer of research, even if you spend the majority of your time providing human services; new research findings will directly influence the way in which you practice psychology. The skills you learn as a graduate student in critical thinking, hypothesizing, and problem solving will be used in almost all research in or applications of psychology in your professional life.

Now let's take a closer look at some of these common ingredients—the activities that you will typically be engaged in as a graduate student. As you read, assess honestly whether the activities appeal to you highly, somewhat, or not at all. If you have negative feelings about any of them now but your aspirations are still strong, ask yourself if there is something you could do to turn those feelings around. For example, if writing papers was your nemesis as an undergraduate, perhaps you could gain confidence in your ability to write by taking (or auditing) a class in composition. In reading about these activities, be honest about your current attitudes but stay open to the possibility of changing them. After all, that is part of what psychology is all about: studying and facilitating change.

Attending Classes

The number and kind of classes you will attend will change as you progress through your program. Initially, you will spend a substantial proportion of your time in foundation courses, such as those in research design, statistics, and the core subject areas for your concentration (concentrations and specializations are described in chapter 3). Students in every program in the department may be taking many of these same courses, so you can be sure that some of these courses will seem less relevant to your particular field of interest than will others. Still, they will provide you with a foundation for your later studies and will give you a broad exposure to the discipline of psychology. Beginning in your second year, you will be able to take more (but not necessarily only) classes in your concentration. Later on, as you become involved in research projects, practica, or internships, you will be attending fewer classes, and those that you do attend will be geared toward intensive training in your concentration and preparing you to complete your thesis, dissertation, or final doctoral project.

The average course load for a doctoral program ranges from 9 to 14 semester hours; the number of classes tends to vary mostly by area of concentration and by year in the program. If this seems like a light load, you should know that classroom experiences are likely to be quite different from those you had as an undergraduate. You will no longer be a face in the crowd, as may have been the case in undergraduate survey courses. (The typical class size in graduate school ranges from 6 to 20 students.) You will be highly visible, and high expectations may be placed on your performance, participation, and professional comportment. Your relationships with fellow students and professors will be closer and qualitatively different. Your professors will not just dispense grades; they will be your advisers and mentors, and, like your classmates, they will be your current and future colleagues.

In addition to your coursework, the core of your learning will come from outside of the classroom—from reading, writing, conducting research, and practicum experiences. A primary purpose of your classes will be to provide a forum in which you can share your questions, expertise, and insights with your colleagues. They will be important resources for your own learning and professional development.

One issue that practically all psychology graduate students have to face is competition. You will be in elite company: None of you would be present if you were not among the best and brightest. For some who aced most courses as an undergraduate with a modicum of effort, this may be quite stressful. There will be courses in which you will feel completely over your head. There will be times when you have to study intensely over a long period just to make a B. There will be students who seem proficient in areas that you haven't begun to grasp. If you are prepared for this, you will not misinterpret your struggle as a sign that you are not graduate psychology material. You will know that it is a natural part of being in a competitive program, and you will approach it as a challenge or a problem to be solved and will apply any number of strategies to solve it.

Reading

Academic psychology is founded on a canon of literature that spans more than 100 years. The largest proportion of your graduate training will revolve around mastering this body of information. One thing that you can be certain of as a graduate student, then, is that you will have to do an extraordinary amount of reading. Usually, professors will assign required reading (several textbooks and numerous articles for each course), but often you will be expected to create your own reading list and to read widely from scholarly books and journals. Your professors will generally be neither checking to see that you have done your reading nor testing your comprehension on a weekly basis. How much and how well you read and comprehend will be your responsibility.

Psychological literature, like that of any science-based discipline, is a highly specialized genre and, therefore, demands special skills. Perhaps the best way to describe the special skills necessary to comprehending psychological texts is to group the information into two categories: the what and the how (or content and methods) of psychology. The what category includes the history of psychological events and ideas, definitions of concepts and theories, and conclusions about the nature and functioning of human behavior. The how of psychology pertains to the scientific tools and techniques that are used to investigate behavioral, cognitive, sensory, and affective phenomena and the theories and techniques that guide professional practice.

Much of what you read will be reports of research that follow a standard format. The author describes initial questions or observations that provoked the study, usually by summing these up in a hypothesis, and reviews pertinent literature. He or she then describes how the study was conducted: the subjects, tools, materials, and procedures used to test the hypothesis. The author then presents the results of the study by reporting the data that were obtained in narrative, statistical, and visual forms. Finally, the author evaluates and interprets the data and states conclusions based on the implications of the data.

Comprehension of such texts cannot be achieved solely by remembering what you have read. You must be able to evaluate the questions being asked, the data obtained, and the methods used in order to judge the accuracy and validity of the conclusions drawn. In other words, you must have excellent critical thinking and analytical reasoning skills.

Writing

You can also expect to do a good deal of writing both during and after graduate school. You will encounter relatively few objective tests (e.g., true–false or multiple choice); most of the tests you do take will be essay tests. The majority of your classes will entail writing papers, and you will be required to report in written form the results of any research projects you are involved in and the progress of your practicum and internship experiences. Many of you will be required to write a thesis or dissertation, which you may eventually revise and submit for publication (see Resources). And throughout your career as a psychologist, whether you are research- or practice-oriented, you will be expected to contribute your knowledge to the field by publishing your findings. You will be required to learn and conform to the conventions outlined in the *Publication Manual of the American Psychological Association* (see Resources). If you absolutely hate to write or are unwilling to acquire good writing skills, you should seriously question whether to pursue a career in psychology: Writing is an essential activity in graduate psychology programs and in most careers based on such degrees.

Public Speaking

In graduate school, class discussion will be more important and oral presentations will be more numerous than they were in undergraduate school. Some presentations will be simple reports of the literature, and others will be of a more integrative nature. You will be expected to digest, write, and then present on a particular topic. You must also be prepared to speak in an impromptu way. Most likely, you will not be "grilled" as some law and medical students are, but you will be expected to take an active role and to articulate your ideas in class, much more so than you were expected to as an undergraduate. Again, as you progress through the semesters with your classmates, together you will help teach the class; your professor will increasingly become a facilitator. For students who have the opportunity to be teaching assistants, public speaking will be even more important. Their duties may include lecturing in undergraduate classes and leading student laboratories. All students completing dissertations will have to present a proposal for their research to their dissertation committee before collecting data and will have to defend their dissertation after it is completed.

Research

How much and what kind of research you do as a graduate student will vary depending on your specific area of study and on the model on which your program is based (see chapter 3). Regardless of the training model and your area of concentration, two things are certain: You will spend a good deal of time in the library, combing the literature, and a variable amount of time in the laboratory or at a research site, actually conducting research. Every doctoral candidate and most master's candidates are required to have foundation courses in research methods, design, and statistics and to apply that knowledge in actual research. Most doctoral programs require a dissertation in which the student performs independent research. Even in some PsyD programs (see chapter 3) that do not require original research as part of the dissertation, you must learn to be a sophisticated consumer of research. This involves considerable expertise in understanding research design and statistics.

Work Experience

Later in your training, you will be required to acquire on-the-job experience that is related to your area of concentration. This will mean, for example, working as a researcher or as an intern in a professional work setting. Whether or not you are paid for this experience, you will be, in essence, an employee in training. These work experiences will give you a chance to apply your education in a formal work setting, and they will give both you and your evaluators the opportunity to assess your professional abilities. You will encounter knotty problems as a researcher: Subjects will drop out, funding may be cut, staff may transfer to another facility, and data will be disappointing. As a clinician, you will be called on to make decisions that will have significant repercussions on others' lives, and you will be expected to do so under stressful circumstances. In addition to your psychological expertise, time management, organization, and your ability to function in a team will be scrutinized. Future employers will base their decision to hire you partly on evaluations of this work.

Step 2.3: Determine Whether You Possess Those Personal Characteristics Known to Contribute to Success

The members of any given profession can be said to share some general characteristics. For example, it might be said that mathematicians thrive on solving problems in systematic and logical ways, that good teachers are able to motivate others to learn, and that athletes are driven by the desire to test the physical limits of the human body. Similarly, it is possible to list certain general characteristics that psychologists, and students of psychology, share. According to some psychology professors, their most successful students are those who are passionately interested in psychology, mature, self-motivated, hard-working, highly organized, full of stamina, and flexible. Successful students are also commonly described as being serious, responsible, committed, curious, focused, and scientifically oriented. In addition, those successful in clinical work are empathetic, have good boundaries, and are able to set firm limits under conditions of duress.

To understand why these particular characteristics are so important, you need only consider the benchmarks of graduate psychology training. Ultimately, you will have to take comprehensive exams and write a thesis or dissertation to receive your degree. At that time, you will be expected to demonstrate that you have an adequate command of the entire body of knowledge that exists in your area of concentration. In your internship, you will be expected to have a keen understanding of any number of psychology-related topics. If you do research, you will have to have a firm grasp of research methodology and statistics as they are applied in your particular area. If you do clinical work, you will likely be dealing with people in crisis who will rely on your expertise about assessment of and treatment for their particular problems.

Your training program is designed to familiarize you with the discipline and to provide access to human and physical resources in the form of professors, classrooms, labs, libraries, training sites, and supervisors. It is entirely up to you to put these resources to use to acquire the knowledge and experience that you need. As we described earlier in this chapter, that knowledge and experience will come from 2 to 4 years (for master's programs) or 4 to 7 years (for doctoral programs) of intensive, self-directed learning—learning in large part garnered by your own reading, writing, research, and practical experiences. Much of this will involve interpreting hundreds of scientific texts and performing or consuming a substantial amount of research. People who are hard-working, self-motivated, passionately interested, scientifically oriented, and so forth will be better suited than others for persisting in such tasks.

In Step 2.2, we described the importance of participating in class, reading, analyzing, writing, public speaking, research, and on-the-job skills. There are also a number of skill-related personal characteristics that are exhibited by hard-working, self-motivated students. To succeed, you must have strong interpersonal skills. You must know how to listen, when and how to be assertive, and how to work with others cooperatively toward a common goal. Successful graduate students are also invariably self-disciplined. You must be able to persevere without supervision or immediate rewards, and to demonstrate good study habits on a consistent basis. The ability to concentrate for long periods of time, to use the library efficiently, to organize your workload well, and to collaborate with students and professors will be necessary for you to make the most efficient use of your time.

In fact, time-management skills might well be the most crucial skills of all. As your graduate school career progresses, increasingly greater demands will be made on your time. Initially, you will be apportioning your time among attending classes (in the lecture hall or in a laboratory), reading, and doing course assignments. Later in the program, you will also be spending time in laboratories or at research sites if your training is research-oriented, preparing for and teaching classes if you are training to teach, and working as an intern if you are training to be a practitioner. In your final year, you may be doing all of this as well as working on your thesis or dissertation. It is no small task to juggle so many activities simultaneously. If you give in to a tendency to procrastinate, you will not survive (see Resources).

In chapter 4, we discuss in more detail what graduate programs are looking for in their candidates, both academically and personally. As you will discover, admissions committees will be searching your application materials for evidence of these highly prized personal characteristics as well as related skills, because they know from experience that these attributes do often go hand-in-hand with success. The purpose of discussing the issue here is to encourage you to begin to assess your personal characteristics as yet another important step in your decision making. If you take the time to understand your own strengths and limitations now, you will be in a better position to communicate your particular strengths to selection committees, and you may be able to build into your timetable strategies to improve on your weaker points.

If you feel that your skills are lacking (e.g., reading, writing, study, or time-management skills), you can take comfort in the knowledge that any of these skills can be learned and improved on if you are committed to doing so. Insofar as personal characteristics are concerned, it may be more of a challenge to change ingrained patterns such as a tendency not to complete projects, an aversion to math, or the need to be always told what to do. People are, however, most highly motivated to change when they have the most to gain from doing so. So our general advice to you is that if you are intensely interested in graduate work in psychology, you may be able to overcome many perceived shortcomings, either through self-discipline alone or with the assistance of a tutor, mentor, or counselor. Use the field you're thinking of going into to your own advantage: There are excellent books and articles based on solid psychological research (a few are listed in the Resources section), and there are trained psychologists who can work with you to address specific problems you fear might hamper you in your graduate work. Having been through graduate school in psychology themselves, many will have an "insider's" view that can be helpful in other ways as well.

If you have come this far in the book but have some doubts about your skills or personal suitability, take cheer from the words of humorist William Allen, who once tried to set a world record for balancing a broom in the palm of his hand: "Talent helps, all right, but in the end what matters is still old-fashioned desire fostered by proper attitude" (Allen, 1986, p. 59).

Step 2.4: Familiarize Yourself With the Realities of Pursuing a Graduate Degree

Up to this point, you have been asked to explore your reasons for considering graduate study, to contemplate the life-style of a graduate psychology student, and to examine your skills and personal suitability for such a life. Now let's turn to some of the practical implications of graduate study that may influence your final decision to apply.

Admission Standards and Competition

We will go into much detail about assessing your qualifications for admission to a particular program in chapter 4. The purpose of this section is to familiarize you with the general criteria that are used by selection committees, so that you have a realistic overview of how applicants are typically evaluated.

A variety of criteria are used by graduate programs to evaluate applicants for both master's and doctoral programs in psychology. The kind of criteria and the emphasis placed on each varies from program to program. Many programs look first at your grade point average (GPA) and at your scores on the Verbal, Quantitative, Analytical, and Subject portions of the Graduate Record Exam (GRE) and on the Miller Analogies Test (MAT). Almost all programs require personal essays and letters of recommendation, and some value them as much as they do the GPA and test scores. Specific undergraduate coursework (such as statistics, laboratory-based experimental courses, and history and systems) may be required. Many programs also prize diversity in their student population, and to gain such diversity they will look at GPA and test scores in the context of the other assets that a particular student might bring.

On the average, the minimum GPA required to gain serious consideration for a doctoral program in psychology is 3.2. For master's programs, a 3.0 GPA is recommended. However, programs may place different emphasis on overall undergraduate GPA, the last 2 years' GPA, or the psychology GPA. The average minimum GRE score (on any portion) required to be competitive for doctoral programs is 550 and for master's programs is 500, but note that not all programs use the analytical score or the psychology subject score in evaluating applicants. We emphasize that these are average minimums, which means that currently the majority of programs have set 3.2 as their minimum GPA requirement and 550 as their minimum GRE requirement for doctoral applicants, for example. Many programs do set higher minimums, many set "preferred" minimums as well, and most programs will change their minimums for a particular pool of applicants (e.g., if the pool is very large and most applicants have superior grades and scores, minimums may be raised to reduce the eligible pool; if diversity is a strong value, GRE scores and GPAs may be evaluated in the context of other qualifications). Additionally, programs use any number of the additional selection criteria: letters of recommendation, personal essays, the quality of coursework, interviews, previous research activities, psychology-related work experience, clinically related public service, and extracurricular activities.

The Application Process

As you may have guessed from the timetables in chapter 1 and Appendix A, applying to graduate school is a more complex process than applying to most undergraduate programs. However, both involve strict adherence to deadlines and the payment of nonrefundable fees. Most psychology graduate programs set deadlines for receiving applications for fall enrollment between February 1 and March 1 of the same year; again, this varies from school to school (e.g., some have deadlines in January, and others have deadlines in April; some programs for students who wish to respecialize have rolling admissions). Most of the time, these deadlines are absolutely nonnegotiable, and partially completed applications will not be considered. For every application filed, an application fee must be paid (approximately $40 each, as of 1993) as well as a fee for transcripts and test scores. If you are applying to 10 or more schools, this can quickly add up. And some schools invite finalists to preselection interviews (see chapter 7); the expenses most often must be borne by the applicant.

As you saw in chapter 1, there are quite a few tasks that must be completed in a relatively short period of time to complete an application. Some of the tasks are tedious. They will require your utmost in terms of organization, persistence, and follow-through. Most of the tasks are anxiety provoking. They will require that you persevere despite apprehension.

Students who are members of specific populations may find that the process is even more challenging or that it requires additional steps. Returning students (i.e., those who have been out of undergraduate school for a number of years), for example, must find ways to update their credentials and obtain appropriate letters of recommendation without having the kind of resources those still in school do. Students who already have a master's degree in psychology will need to carefully research whether programs will accept any of their course credits or whether they will, in essence, be starting over again. Students with disabilities will need to make sure the campus and program environments accommodate their disability. Respecialization students (i.e., those with a doctorate in one area of psychology who wish to gain credentials in another) will need to speak with representatives of programs before submitting their applications. International students must document their abilities to write and speak the English language at an advanced level, and may need to take additional application steps. Those who want to do research with or provide services to members of particular populations (e.g., women, lesbians and gay men, and ethnic minorities) must ascertain whether a particular program has appropriate faculty and would generally be hospitable in that regard. In chapters 5 and 6, we discuss all of these additional aspects further in the context of choosing and applying to programs.

The Costs of a Graduate School Education

It typically takes a full-time student 4 to 7 years to earn a doctorate in psychology and 2 to 4 years to earn a master's degree. In most doctoral programs, you must attend full-time, and during most of that time, graduate study will truly be more than a full-time job.[1] Therefore, most programs strongly urge you not to work at an outside job, either full- or

---

1. Some, but not all, PsyD programs allow part-time study, at least during part of their training.

part-time. Some (but not all) master's programs do allow you to attend part-time, and in that case a part-time job can be accommodated.

If you are currently working at a well-paying job, giving up that income for a number of years may be a consideration in deciding whether to go to graduate school and which degree to pursue. Likewise, if you are working at a satisfying job in which you are gaining valuable experience, you will need to consider whether the benefits of going to graduate school full-time outweigh the career costs of resigning from that position. Should you decide that pursuing full-time graduate study is worth it, you will find that wholeheartedly involving yourself in graduate school will more than make up for the sacrifice.

The average cost of a year's tuition at the time this book goes to press is estimated at $5,800, although at some schools it can be as low as $2,000 and at others as high as $12,000. With the cost of books and supplies estimated at approximately $200 a semester, the average academic costs are over $6,000 a year. Depending on the cost of living in a particular geographical area (i.e., factoring in the costs of food, lodging, and supplies), the price for a year of graduate study can be quite high.

Fortunately, there are quite a few financial aid strategies you can pursue, which are described in chapters 5 and 6. The purpose of citing costs now is to encourage you to weigh the money factor in with all of the other factors as you consider whether to apply to graduate school in psychology. We urge you not to make finances your primary consideration at this point, however, particularly if you are typically very cost conscious. There are many creative ways to finance graduate school for the person who is willing to do his or her homework (again, see chapters 5 and 6). And, when you do reflect on costs, also think about the considerable earning power you will have once you have acquired your degree.

Employment Outlook

The employment prospects for graduate-degree holders in psychology are generally quite good, in terms of both employment rates and salaries. Statistics from 1991 show that 98% of new doctorates were employed: 75% were employed full-time, 10% were employed part-time, and nearly 11% were employed as postdoctoral fellows. Only 2% of all female doctoral recipients and 1% of all male recipients were unemployed and seeking employment. Employment rates did not vary significantly by area of concentration. For some ethnic minorities, unemployment rates were even lower, in part because of the urgent need for psychologists who are qualified to provide services to minority populations (minority students are still underrepresented in doctoral programs in psychology and have constituted only 11% of those receiving doctorates over the last 10 years). Women continue to increase in numbers in the field, receiving 61% of the doctorates awarded in 1991.

Of the employed graduates, just over half found employment before receiving the doctorate, and another 15% found employment within 3 months of receiving the doctorate; 8% took up to 6 months. Full-time employment rates were nearly even for those employed in service provider fields versus research fields: 76% of health service provider doctoral recipients were employed full-time, and 74% of research doctorates were employed full-time (Kohout & Wicherski, 1993).[2]

Typical salaries vary according to the kind of position acquired and the degree, and depend on the level of experience. In 1991, for faculty positions, the median salary for doctoral-level faculty was $45,000; for master's-level faculty (of which there were far fewer), the median salary was $35,000. For doctoral-level educational administrators, the median salary was $67,000; at the master's level it was $55,000. For research positions at the doctoral level, the median salary was $50,000; at the master's level this was $48,000 (Kohout & Wicherski, 1992).

Salaries for positions involving direct human services varied a great deal. For doctoral-level clinical psychologists, salaries ranged from $10,000 to $282,000, with a median of $53,000. At the master's level, the median was $40,000. In counseling psychology, the range was $18,000 to $180,000 for those with a doctoral degree, with a median of $48,000. At the master's level, the median was $37,000. Doctoral-level school psychologists earned from $23,000 to $130,000, with a median of $55,000. At the master's level, the median was $52,000 (Kohout & Wicherski, 1992).

In applied psychology, doctoral-level industrial/organizational psychologists earned a median of $76,000; those in other types of applied psychology had a median income of $66,000. The median income in applied psychology was $55,000 for those at the master's level. The highest salaries were in the administration of applied psychology—for example, managing an organization or consulting firm specializing in industrial/organizational psychology or market research. Salaries here ranged

---

2. These data and those that follow are from surveys conducted by the APA's Office of Demographic, Employment, and Educational Research (ODEER). For updates of these data, contact that office at 202-336-5980 or write to ODEER, American Psychological Association, 750 First Street, NE, Washington, DC 20002.

from $30,000 to $300,000, with a median of $84,000, at the doctoral level. At the master's level, the median was $50,000 (Kohout & Wicherski, 1992).

Conclusion

In this chapter, we have tried to give you a realistic overview of the first step of the application process: beginning to assess whether a graduate degree in psychology is the right choice for you. We have encouraged you to examine your motivation and to assess whether you have (or could gain) the interest and skills necessary to meet the academic demands of graduate school. We have asked you to consider the admission standards and competition, the application process itself, the costs in time and money of attending graduate school, and the employment outlook for psychologists.

We hope that you don't consider doubts at this point as evidence that you shouldn't apply. Many potential applicants experience marked ambivalence at this stage, and it may help to know that this is a normal part of the process. (In fact, having *no* doubts might be a cause for concern. You may not have been honest with yourself or allowed the information to really sink in.) We encourage you to see doubts as challenges to gain further information, some of which will be provided in the following chapters of this book and some of which can be obtained through diligence on your part. In any case, by continuing to read, you give yourself the benefit of the doubt, which in this case means you allow yourself to have all the necessary information to make an informed decision. That way, you will be less likely to regret your decision later.

In the next chapter, we take a break from looking at challenges and begin to look at all of the options you will have in pursuing a graduate degree in psychology. As you will see, psychology is truly a flexible science and profession, one that offers much variety and is able to meet the needs of many people. As you read, we hope that you will be better able to decide for yourself if you can truly "spend your life your own way" by pursuing a career in this field.

Decisions to Make Before Researching Graduate Programs in Psychology

The shoe that fits one person pinches another; there is no recipe . . . that suits all cases.—Carl Jung

Success in any field is in large part determined by the degree of fit between the individual and the occupational tasks. In this chapter, we would like to help you get a clearer sense of what psychologists actually do so that you can gauge the fit between you and a particular area of psychology. You may be enticed by such job titles as "sports psychologist," "neuropsychological researcher," "human factors engineer," and "play therapist." These titles reflect some of the variety in the field of psychology. Knowledge of careers in psychology and of the degree options that lead to them is essential to making choices about particular programs. For example, have you thought about

- whether you see yourself primarily as a researcher, as a practitioner, or as some combination of both?
- what type of setting you want to work in?
- what kinds of activities you see yourself doing from day to day?
- which of the more than 100 areas of psychology you want to concentrate on?
- which degree you should earn to obtain employment in your chosen field?
- whether it is necessary to enroll in an accredited program?
- whether you will need licensure or certification?

Although many who have a doctoral or a master's degree in psychology continue to work in traditional settings (e.g., higher education and human services) and to fill traditional roles (e.g., researcher, practitioner, or both), there are increasingly more and varied options both for studying and for practicing psychology. The purpose of this chapter is to help you sort through the myriad of options and narrow them down thoughtfully. In that way, you will be more prepared to research particular programs and will be less likely to feel overwhelmed when you begin looking at the over 600 programs offering graduate degrees in psychology. To begin this exploration, it is useful to get an overview of the field of psychology and to see how your interests fit in.

What Is Psychology?

If you are reading this book, you must have considerable interest in psychology. But like many people, you may be hard pressed to define exactly what psychology is and what a variety of jobs psychologists do. Although society's understanding of psychology is probably better now than it has ever been, confusion and controversy about the discipline still prevail.

Webster's dictionary defines psychology primarily as "the science of mind and behavior" and secondarily as "the study of mind and behavior in relation to a particular field of knowledge or activity." The first definition reflects the traditional view of psychology as being exclusively a science. The second definition reflects the more contemporary reality that psychology is both a science and a profession and that psychology can involve basic research or can be applied in many areas. It is important to understand this dual nature of psychology because you will encounter it many times while you are investigating your career options, while you are shopping for a graduate program, and throughout your career.

As a formal academic discipline in the United States, psychology is just over 100 years old. The first training grounds for psychologists were university laboratories in Europe, and most of psychology at the time was experimental. Perception, sensation, learning, and memory were among the many phenomena that were studied. This tradition of basic research continues today among many experimental psychologists.

Early on, psychologists, particularly in the United States, began to see real-world applications for their research. For example, knowledge gained from experiments in learning could be used to develop and improve teaching methods. When other applications began to proliferate, however, they were not unanimously viewed with seriousness by the public. In 1924, noted humorist Stephen Leacock wrote,

> In the earlier days this science was kept strictly confined to the colleges. . . . It had no particular connection with anything at all, and did no visible harm to those who studied it. . . . All this changed. As part of the new researches, it was found that psychology can be used . . .

for almost everything in life. There is now not only psychology in the academic or college sense, but also a Psychology of Business, Psychology of Education, a Psychology of Playing the Banjo.... For almost every juncture of life we now call in the services of an expert psychologist as naturally as we send for an emergency plumber. In all our great cities there are already, or soon will be, signs that read "Psychologist—Open Day and Night." (cited in Benjamin, 1986, pp. 943–944)

The American public's understanding of, respect for, and demand for psychology fluctuated during its first 50 years. In the earliest days, as Leacock's commentary illustrates, applied psychology was often viewed with suspicion. Although clinical psychology, in the form of psychodiagnostics, had been practiced from the earliest days of psychology in America, it was mainly after psychologists achieved success in working with battle-fatigued World War I veterans that respect for that discipline surged. However, it flagged again during the Great Depression when people lost faith that psychologists could help alleviate serious economic and morale problems of the times.

World War II marked a critical turning point for both applied and clinical psychology in the United States. The war work of psychologists was highly praised by government, industry, and the military, and the discipline was firmly established as a profession that could exist alongside research in academe.[1]

Today, the expertise of psychology graduates of all kinds is again in healthy demand. For traditional researchers, applied psychologists, and especially clinicians, many doors are open, but graduates with more unusual specialties are finding niches as well. Nowadays it is not uncommon to find psychologists being summoned, for example, to the site of a hijacking or a natural disaster. Psychologists are not only present in universities and clinics, but also in business, government, the military, and the courts. Ironically, Leacock's prediction has come true: There is a real demand for "Psychologist: Open Day or Night."

We have provided this admittedly brief history to give you a context for the discussion about settings, training models, and areas of concentration in psychology that follows. For more comprehensive accounts of

---

1. There has often been conflict over psychology's status as a science and as a profession. This tension has been reflected in the major organization serving psychology, the APA. If you are interested in the continuing debate over science versus practice, Hilgard's (1987) chapter "The Professional Organization of Psychologists: Scholars and Practitioners" provides a good introduction.

Exhibit 3.1

Typical Work Settings for Psychology Graduates

Academic Settings

- University
  - Academic department
  - Management or administrative office
  - Professional school (e.g., psychology, business, law, medicine, or dentistry)
  - Research center or institute
- Four-year college
  - Academic department
  - Management or administrative office
  - Research center or institute
- Two-year college (e.g., community college or technical college)
- University-affiliated professional school
- Freestanding professional school
- Adult education program
- Elementary or secondary school
- School system administrative office
- Special education or vocational school

Human Service Settings

- Outpatient clinic
  - Community mental health center
  - Health maintenance organization
- Hospital
  - Public general hospital
  - Private general hospital
  - Public psychiatric hospital
  - Nonprofit private psychiatric hospital
  - For-profit, private psychiatric hospital
  - Military hospital
  - VA hospital
- Independent practice
  - Individual private practice
  - Group psychological practice
  - Medical/psychology group practice
- Other
  - Health service for specific groups
  - Nonuniversity counseling and guidance centers
  - University/college counseling and guidance centers
  - Nursing home or other skilled-care facility
  - Training centers for people with mental retardation

continued

Exhibit 3.1, continued

Business Settings

- Business or industry
- Consulting firm
- Independent research organization or laboratory
- Industrial/organizational psychology practice
- Associations
- Self-employed

Government and Military Settings

- Armed services
- Civil service
- Criminal justice system
- Elected office
- Federal, state, or local government agency
- Government research organization (e.g., National Institute of Mental Health)

the history of psychology in the United States, see Hilgard (1987) and Koch and Leary (1992). For a history of psychotherapy, see Freedheim et al. (1992). Evans, Sexton, and Cadwallader (1992) provide a historical account of the major organization serving psychologists throughout the United States, the APA.

Where Do Psychologists Work? What Do Psychologists Do?

Psychologists work in virtually every setting imaginable. This is not surprising, because psychology is a science of mind and behavior, and these exist wherever people (and other animals) are found. Exhibit 3.1 illustrates the variety of settings in which psychologists typically work. Before you begin researching programs, it may be helpful for you to get a sense of the general environment in which you wish to work (e.g., medical, academic, private practice, or business). Employment in some settings will necessitate your having a particular specialty, concentration, or degree, and perhaps a license.

The kinds of work performed by psychologists can be as varied as their work settings; however, there are four realms of activity that psychologists typically engage in: teaching, research, scholarly writing, and providing psychological services directly to clients (individuals, families, groups, and organizations). Psychologists differ in the amount of time (if any) they spend in each of these activities. Clinical psychologists who teach and do research in a university setting while maintaining a private practice and publishing periodically would be involved in all four, for example, but might differ in the amount of time they spend in each. A human factors engineer may work for a large aerospace corporation, performing and applying research, while teaching part-time at a university. Psychologists also differ in the extent to which they specialize in researching or serving a particular population (e.g., women, members of ethnic minorities, gay men and lesbians). We talk more about this last aspect in chapter 5.

It is useful for you to begin to decide what percentage of your time you wish to spend in any one of these realms once you have completed your degree. That way, you can choose a graduate program now that best trains you to work in the manner you'd like to work later. Some programs are heavily research oriented, whereas others emphasize combined practice and research. Accordingly, graduate programs differ as to how much coursework and experience is devoted to the four realms of activity we described earlier. These differences can be conceptualized in part by considering contemporary models of training and practice in psychology.[2]

Three Models of Training and Practice in Psychology

Originally, there was only one model of training and practice in psychology: the research scientist model. But as people became more interested in being practitioners and the public's demand for practitioner services grew, a need was seen for training that was geared more specifically to practice. Two other models emerged: the scientist–practitioner model and the professional model.

These three models not only represent the manner in which psychologists are trained, but also may reflect the manner in which they work after completing graduate training. Generally speaking, these models represent the extent to which training or employment in psychology

2. We are indebted to Heidi L. Alletzhauser and Stephen C. McConnell, who graciously contributed from their unpublished manuscript, "The Doctor of Psychology Degree: A Guide for Prospective Students (1993)," many of the ideas and much of the information contained in the following section on training models.

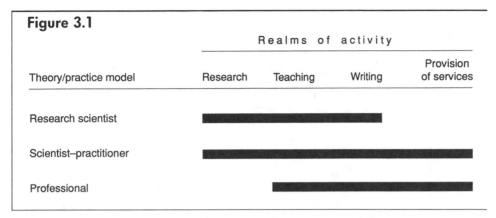

Figure 3.1

Focus of activity in three models of training and practice in psychology.

focuses either on research activities or on the provision of services. If you think of the three models as three points plotted on a graph moving from pure research to pure practice, then at one end the research scientist is most focused on research, at the other end the professional is most focused on practice, and the scientist–practitioner lies somewhere in between. Using the four broad realms of activity listed earlier, Figure 3.1 illustrates how the realms of activity overlap across the three models. Because your choice of model is important, both in selecting graduate programs and in plotting your career path, it is essential that you understand clearly the differences among the three models.

The Research Scientist Model

What does the term "research scientist" call to mind? Do you picture a person clad in a white lab coat, scribbling notes on a clipboard while watching rats learn to negotiate a maze? As with all stereotypes, there are psychology researchers who do actually fit this description. But you can also find researchers in a "laboratory" such as a courtroom, the site of a tornado, a hospital, or a pharmaceutical firm. And although rats are still valuable subjects, researchers usually study human behavior and related artifacts, such as tape recordings of speech patterns and brain scan tomography.

A primary orientation toward research is the most distinguishing characteristic of this model. Research scientists are scholars, and most often teachers, who divide their time among conducting research in their specialty field, writing about their findings, and teaching. What motivates research scientists is the desire to learn more about the mind and behavior through experimental methods, to contribute such knowledge to helping individuals and groups solve problems, and to teach what they have learned to others.

Psychology researchers have made significant contributions to science. It was a psychologist who discovered that the autonomic and central nervous systems are connected, not separate, as was formerly believed. This knowledge led to the creation of biofeedback and behavioral medicine, which, in turn, have helped scores of people overcome physical and mental health problems. Our educational system is still largely based on pioneering studies undertaken by learning theorists earlier in this century. Our understanding of the growth and development of infants and children was changed radically by psychologists who devoted their lifetimes to studying them. As a result, education, parenting, and medical care for infants and children underwent revolutionary changes.

Training in the research scientist model focuses on supplying students with the knowledge and tools necessary for scientific investigation. Typically, students are given rigorous training in the use of research methods and are required to complete coursework in some of the core subject areas of psychology, which may include perception, sensation, learning, memory, personality, motivation, and quantitative, developmental, physiological, and social psychology. With this foundation, students are expected to take additional courses in one or more subjects that will become their areas of concentration and to begin to perform research in those areas as soon as possible. How early and to what extent students focus primarily on these areas of concentration varies from program to program.

According to 1991 data, 8% of new psychology doctorate recipients were employed in careers focusing almost exclusively on research. A sizable number of these researchers were employed in universities (31%), and a majority (52%) were employed in business and government settings (Kohout & Wicherski, 1993). It should be noted, however, that a much larger percentage of new graduates than 8% are typically involved in research as part of their professional lives. Although the number of psychology doctorate recipients pursuing clinical careers has increased considerably, the research market is still highly viable. Forecasters expect the demand for research scientists to remain stable and perhaps even increase as the current generation of academics begins to retire.

The Scientist–Practitioner Model

Around the 1930s, two trends emerged. Psychologists began to see increased applications for their laboratory findings, and they became significantly more interested in providing human services. Concurrently, society's acceptance of and demand for practitioner services was growing. With its almost exclusive focus on experimentation, the traditional research scientist training model was seen by many as being inadequate for training practitioners, particularly in the area of clinical psychology but in other areas as well.

At a historic conference held in Boulder, Colorado, in 1949, a new model was officially endorsed for clinicians: the scientist–practitioner model (often called the Boulder model). This model is designed to provide a grounding in research methods and a breadth of exposure to psychology. Its goals are to (a) provide more practitioner-oriented coursework and experiences than does the research scientist model; (b) train practitioners to conduct and consume research of both an applied and an experimental nature, for the specific purpose of enhancing knowledge and practice of clinical and applied psychology; and (c) guide practitioners in applying the skills of science to applied activities, such as assessment and treatment. Programs following this model generally require more course hours in applied and clinical subjects and more experience in internships and practica in applied and clinical settings than do programs following the research scientist model. Although the scientist–practitioner model is often used in clinical psychology training programs, it is also prevalent in other areas, such as counseling, school, and industrial/organizational psychology.

A generic description of a scientist–practitioner in clinical psychology might be written as follows: a provider of psychological services—most typically, psychotherapy or counseling—who works in a clinical setting such as a hospital, clinic, or independent practice and who conducts or supervises research, does scholarly writing on clinical issues, and teaches or engages in clinical supervision. As the term "scientist–practitioner" suggests, the framers of the Boulder model expected students of such programs to have both science and practice skills. However, surveys of graduates of these programs indicate that, in reality, many do not have the opportunity to use their research skills as frequently as their practice ones.[3] It is important to note, however, that most clinical psychologists "were involved in some form of research in the recent past, consume a good deal of research, have positive attitudes toward research, and think that research ought to be a continued part of clinical training" (Barrom, Shadis, & Montgomery, 1988, p. 100).

Scientist–practitioner training is characterized by core courses in both basic and applied psychology, supervision during extensive applied or clinical experience, research consumption, and an emphasis on the application of the skills of science that are fundamental to the practice of psychology. This model is an "integrative" one in which "scientist practitioners in psychology reflect a research orientation in their practice and a practice relevance in their research" (Preamble, 1990, p. 4). For example, in treating a client (be it an individual, family, group, or organization), the scientist–practitioner would use scientific skills such as generating hypotheses about the causes of the client's difficulty, operationalizing variables that would be pertinent to treatment, devising or using interventions that have a scientific basis, and testing hypotheses in, and empirically evaluating the results of, interventions.

An important advantage of scientist–practitioner training programs is that they are typically based in university psychology departments, which offer opportunities for interdisciplinary studies and provide quality facilities, such as libraries with extensive holdings. Scientist–practitioner programs are mostly staffed with full-time faculty who are themselves scientist–practitioners involved in teaching, research, and clinical and applied work. This helps to ensure that professional training will be integrated with scientific and research training.

A crucial fact for those considering training in the scientist–practitioner model is that as a graduate student you will be required to perform

---

3. One survey of graduate students enrolled in scientist–practitioner programs revealed that the majority of these students had a predominately clinical orientation and spent about four times as many hours on clinical work as on research (Parker & Detterman, 1988). Another study of clinicians confirmed that the majority spent more time on practice than on research-related activities (Barrom, Shadish, & Montgomery, 1988). The reasons why scientist–practitioners have not been dividing their time equally between research and practice have themselves been a subject of research. Interested readers should see Haynes, Lemsky, and Sexton-Radek (1987) and Barrom et al. (1988).

as well as to consume psychological research. Through this training you will be qualified to provide a variety of services in a wide range of employment settings. You should be aware that how your time will actually be apportioned in terms of research after graduation will be influenced by your work setting and job-related factors as well as by your own desires and your commitment to research. If the combination of research and practice appeals to you, the scientific–professional training offered through many psychology departments may be the model for you.

The Professional Model

In 1973, a third model of study and practice was affirmed at a conference in Vail, Colorado. The Vail model, also known as the professional model or practitioner model, was intended to offer yet another path of study for those whose sole interest was in clinical practice. There are several features that differentiate the professional model from the other two. First, professional training is more strongly focused on clinical practice than are either of the other two models. Second, many (but not all) professional training programs grant a PsyD degree rather than a PhD or EdD degree (see our discussion of degrees later in this chapter). Third, students in some programs that award the PsyD may be allowed to complete an academic project instead of a traditional dissertation. Fourth, admission criteria for professional programs may place more emphasis on the personal qualities of applicants and their clinically related work experience than do those of the other two models. Finally, professional training programs are housed in a greater variety of institutional settings than are research scientist or scientist–practitioner programs.

University-based professional schools are considered by some to be the optimal setting for professional programs. Similar to schools of medicine and law, some of these programs are separate schools within a university and have a great deal of administrative autonomy. In addition, university-based schools have the advantages of access to facilities such as libraries and counseling centers and closer contact with other disciplines within the university. Some PsyD programs are based in university psychology departments, departments that may also grant research-oriented PhDs. Psychology-department-based professional schools may have far less autonomy than do university-based schools, and when a PhD and a PsyD program reside in the same department, there can be competition for resources. On the other hand, department-based professional schools offer students the opportunity to work with a greater variety of psychologists, to be exposed to a much broader content of psychology, and to become familiar with more models of the science and profession of psychology.

Freestanding professional schools are usually private institutions that are autonomous from both psychology departments and universities, and they are probably the most controversial.[4] Common criticisms of freestanding professional schools are as follows: Library facilities may be inadequate; programs may be too isolated from related disciplines; some rely too heavily on tuition for funding; in many, faculty members frequently come from the practice community and teach only part-time, and it is argued that part-time faculty may have less invested in teaching and may not have a great investment in overall program quality; and it is more difficult to assess the quality and accountability of freestanding professional schools than that of university-affiliated schools. Applicants should be aware that these criticisms may apply to only *some* professional schools that are freestanding. Students interested in a freestanding professional school can inquire about any of these aspects that are of concern to them when they are investigating their program options (see chapter 5).

There are also several advantages that freestanding professional schools may have. Many are able to admit more students per year, and therefore their admission standards may be more flexible. They may value life experiences more and hence may be more attractive to returning students. Because professional programs stress active contact with practicing professionals more than do other models, they may provide a greater number of clinician role models. Professional schools offer a more strictly practice-oriented curriculum and may be more supportive of students who have already decided that their primary career goal is practice. Finally, some professional schools may allow for some degree of part-time enrollment, a rarity in doctoral programs following the scientist–practitioner model.

Like scientist–practitioner training, professional training is characterized by core courses in both basic and applied psychology, supervision during extensive clinical experience, and research consumption. Both require predoctoral internships that are usually full-time appointments

---

4. In 1987, The National Conference on Graduate Education recommended that after 1995 all freestanding schools be university-affiliated to be accredited by the APA, and many do see a trend toward university affiliation.

Table 3.1

Employment Picture as Reported by 1991 PhD and PsyD Recipients in Clinical Psychology

Perception/Status	PhD		PsyD	
	N	%	*N*	%
Total, all respondents	720	100.0	241	100.0
Perception of Job Market				
Bleak	12	1.7	8	3.3
Poor	85	11.8	35	14.5
Fair	298	41.4	89	36.9
Good	257	35.7	79	32.8
Excellent	64	8.9	25	10.4
Not specified	4	0.6	5	2.1
Employment status				
Employed full-time	507	70.4	186	77.2
Employed part-time	107	14.9	26	10.8
Postdoc fellow	83	11.5	23	9.5
Unemployed seeking	13	1.8	1	0.4
Unemployed not seeking	10	1.4	1	0.4
Not specified	0	0.0	4	1.7

Note. Column percentages may not total to 100.0% because of rounding. Adapted from Kohout and Wicherski (1993), *1991 Doctorate Employment Survey*. Compiled by the Office of Demographic, Employment, and Educational Research, APA Education Directorate.

in universities, medical centers, community mental health centers, or hospitals. In programs that follow either model of training, students must go through an application process to prospective internships not unlike that of applying to graduate school.

Because the professional model is relatively new and still undergoing refinement, a number of studies have been undertaken to assess the quality of training this model provides. One comparison of PsyD interns in professional training programs and their clinical PhD counterparts in scientist–practitioner programs showed no significant differences between the two groups in terms of core clinical skills and professional competence, with one exception: PhD interns approached problems more systemically and less intuitively than did PsyD interns, and PsyD interns seemed to be more aware of the feelings and beliefs of others than were PhD interns (Snepp & Peterson, 1988).

Table 3.2

Level of Satisfaction With Current Position Reported (by Percentage) by Employed 1991 PhD and PsyD Recipients in Clinical Psychology

Factor/degree	Very satisfied	Satis-fied	Dissat-isfied	Very dissatis-fied	Not ap-plicable
Salary					
PhD	9.9	49.2	28.0	11.1	0.8
PsyD	13.2	45.8	31.1	9.9	0.0
Benefits					
PhD	22.1	41.5	16.1	9.4	10.1
PsyD	19.8	45.8	15.1	8.5	10.4
Opportunities for promotion					
PhD	6.0	37.9	27.4	10.3	17.4
PsyD	5.7	39.2	25.0	9.4	20.3
Opportunities for personal de-velopment					
PhD	24.6	46.1	19.5	6.2	2.8
PsyD	24.5	43.9	22.2	7.1	2.4
Opportunities for recognition					
PhD	17.9	51.5	19.4	6.2	3.9
PsyD	16.0	50.9	22.2	4.7	5.2
Supervisor					
PhD	29.0	42.2	11.1	5.5	10.9
PsyD	28.3	40.6	15.1	6.1	9.4
Colleagues					
PhD	31.8	50.7	9.1	2.0	5.5
PsyD	31.6	49.5	9.4	1.9	7.5
Working condi-tions					
PhD	23.5	49.5	20.0	4.7	1.0
PsyD	22.6	54.7	17.0	4.7	0.0

Note. Row percentages may not total to 100.0% because of rounding. Adapted from Kohout and Wicherski (1993), *1991 Doctorate Employment Survey*. Compiled by the Office of Demographic, Employment, and Educational Research, APA Education Directorate.

The number of students opting for a PsyD degree through a professional program appears to be growing. According to a 1991 survey, 500 PsyD degrees were granted, which constituted approximately 15% of all psychology doctoral degrees granted that year. In 1981, PsyD degrees represented only 7% of all doctoral degrees. The employment rate for PsyD graduates is also encouraging, as shown for clinical psychologists in Table 3.1. For example, 77% of 1991 PsyD graduates in clinical psychology reported full-time employment, compared with 70% for PhD clinical graduates (Kohout & Wicherski, 1993). (Note that many psychologists choose part-time employment willingly.) Table 3.2 compares the career satisfaction of clinical psychologists with PhDs and PsyDs on eight variables. As can be seen, levels of job satisfaction were similar for those with either degree (Kohout & Wicherski, 1993).

Which Model Is Right for You?

In general, if you are interested primarily in research, the research scientist training model may be your best choice. If you are interested in both doing research and practicing, the scientist–practitioner model may be best. If you want to be a clinician or applied practitioner foremost, you have two options: the scientist–practitioner model and the professional model. There are many excellent programs that follow both of these models, and we have discussed some of the potential advantages of each. For those whose primary interest is in practice, the quality of a particular program may be more important than which of these two training models it follows. Good programs following either model are apt to be more alike than different.

When you read program materials or graduate school handbooks (such as *Grad Study*), you may or may not find explicit mention of these models. There are several ways in which you can determine the orientation of a program, however. You can examine the course descriptions and requirements in program materials (see chapter 5) to ascertain how much time you will be required to spend on traditional core and research-oriented subjects, as compared with time required for applied subjects. You can look to see what kind and how much fieldwork, practicum, or internship is required and in what settings. If you can't find out a program's training model through *Grad Study* or materials sent by the program, perhaps the best way to discover the orientation of a program is to talk to professors who teach there or students who are or have been

Exhibit 3.2

Psychology Program Descriptions Illustrating Orientation Toward Research and Practice

Nova University, Ft. Lauderdale, FL
School of Psychology

Programs compared: clinical PhD, clinical PsyD

Degree requirements: PhD: 110 semester hrs., one computer language, predissertation research, dissertation, clinical competence. PsyD: 107 semester hrs., dissertation, clinical competence. All students are required to complete a one-year clinical internship.

Orientation: Clinical and applied developmental PhD programs provide training for doctoral candidates pursuing careers as applied researchers. Equally strong is the commitment to provide training for the practitioner-oriented psychologist. The PsyD program in clinical psychology provides quality training for doctoral candidates committed to the practice of psychology.

Comments: It can be inferred from this description that Nova differentiates a scientist–practitioner model (its PhD) from a professional model (its PsyD), yet *both* offer opportunities for the practitioner-oriented psychologist.

Yale University, New Haven, CT
Department of Psychology

Programs compared: MS(T) and PhD—clinical, cognitive, developmental, psychobiology, and social–personality; master of philosophy

Degree requirements: MS: three basic-level courses, two of which are outside area of concentration; statistics; research methodology; research experience. Students are expected to take at least 8 term courses and 2 semesters of research. PhD: three basic-level courses, two of which are outside area of concentration; data analysis; predissertation research project; essay in area of concentration; dissertation prospectus; dissertation area paper; dissertation; dissertation defense. Master of philosophy: same requirements as for PhD except dissertation and dissertation-related requirements. Not a terminal degree.

Orientation: The chief goal is the training of research workers in academic and applied settings who will broaden the basic scientific knowledge on which the discipline of psychology rests. Major emphasis is given to preparation for research; a definite effort is also made to give students a background for teaching. The concentration on research and teaching is consistent with a variety of career objectives apart from traditional academics (i.e., industrial, consultation, personnel work, medical institutions, etc.). The department does not offer specific training in these specializations, but rather believes that rigorous and balanced exposure to basic psychology is the best preparation for applied psychology. The first im-

continued

Exhibit 3.2, continued

portant aspect of graduate training is advanced study of general psychology, including method and psychological theory. The second is specialized training within the framework of the 25 "themes," with emphasis on preparation for research. Third, the student is encouraged to take advantage of opportunities for wider training related to the field of psychology from among the relevant university-wide resources, emphasizing research rather than practice. For the clinical area, research and practica are strongly integrated. Training is geared to the expectation that the majority of our students will have academic careers and research or policy careers in applied settings.

Comments: Yale differentiates a terminal and nonterminal master's degree. Strong orientation toward research implies a research scientist model for all nonclinical programs; clinical programs are clearly in the scientist—practitioner mode, with a greater emphasis on research than on practice.

University of Hawaii, Honolulu, HI
Department of Psychology

Programs compared: PhD—behavioral—neuroscience, clinical, community, developmental, human and animal cognition, social—personality

Degree requirements: Number of course hours varies depending on area of concentration; comprehensive written and oral exams, two courses of statistics and methodology, and dissertation are required. Clinical students must complete a one-year internship.

Orientation: The department is eclectic in orientation, although the primary emphasis has been traditionally behavioral in a philosophical and methodological sense. In addition, some of the faculty have a humanistic orientation. The graduate programs are aimed at training specialized research skills as well as those that we use in both teaching and applied settings. The clinical program is in the scientist—practitioner tradition with selected emphasis on research, practitioner training, or community.

Comments: Emphasis on research versus practice is unclear from this description; it seems to vary with the area of concentration.

Note. These descriptions were excerpted from program data in *Graduate Study in Psychology*, 1992, Washington, DC: American Psychological Association.

in the program (see chapter 5). If you are interested in researching or serving a particular population, you can also inquire about this at that time (again, see chapter 5).

Even if a program overtly states that it operates according to a specific model, different programs using the same model offer research and clinical and applied training in varying proportions. Exhibit 3.2 provides some excerpts from program descriptions to illustrate how different programs describe their orientations.

Choosing an Area of Concentration

In thinking about which model of training and practice best suits you, you have had to think about the kind of work you want to do and the kind of setting you want to work in. All of these decisions will help you to identify programs that will best meet your needs. But you are only partway there; you also need to choose an area of concentration and a degree appropriate to your career goals. Concentration and degree are closely related. Your concentration will be the subject areas of psychology that you are most interested in; the type of degree you earn will influence how and where you use your specialized knowledge and experience.

Areas of concentration can be categorized in several different ways. In a clinical psychology specialization, for example, some areas of concentration relate to the particular population that you want to work with (e.g., adolescents; couples and families; ethnic minorities). (If you are interested in these population-focused subspecialties, it will be important to choose a program that will train you adequately in this regard. See chapters 5 and 6.) Others reflect a theoretical orientation (e.g., behavioral, cognitive, psychodynamic, or humanistic psychology), and still others describe a particular arena in which psychology is used as one approach to treatment or problem solving (e.g., medical or forensic psychology).

As another example, in applied experimental psychology a student might want to concentrate on human factors engineering, perhaps focusing on computer–human interaction. In personality psychology, a student might concentrate on changes in personality during adulthood. In developmental psychology, one student might concentrate on early childhood socialization, whereas another might focus on adjustment to life changes in the elderly. In educational psychology, a person might concentrate on methods of assessment of learning-disabled students. A military psychologist might focus on the interaction of soldiers and weapon systems or on human behavior under conditions of wartime stress.

If you want to get an idea of how many and what kinds of areas of concentration and emphases exist, take a look at the "Index of Programs by Area of Study Offered" in *Grad Study*. In a recent edition, programs were listed under at least 135 different areas. Although it is not possible to describe such a large number of options in detail here, we provide below thumbnail sketches and some information about typical work settings for several specialties (i.e., clinical, counseling, school, and industrial/organizational psychology) as well as 12 common areas of concentration.

Specialties and Areas of Concentration

The APA recognizes only clinical, counseling, school, and industrial/organizational psychology as "specialties." Other areas are considered "areas of concentrations" or "subfields." They are considered here together.[5]

Clinical Psychology

Clinical psychologists assess and treat people's mental and emotional disorders. Such problems may range from the normal psychological crises related to life-cycle adjustment to extreme conditions such as schizophrenia, personality disorders, or depression. Many clinical psychologists also conduct research or function as consultants, supervisors, or administrators. Clinical psychologists work in both academic institutions and health care settings such as clinics, hospitals, and community mental health centers, as well as in private practice. Many focus their interests on special populations (e.g., children, the elderly) or specific problem areas (such as phobias, substance abuse, or depression).

Counseling Psychology

Closely related to the clinical psychologist is the counseling psychologist. Counseling psychologists, however, are oriented to life span issues such as career development and adjustment, marriage and family counseling, and a variety of other issues associated with problems encountered by most people during their life span. These psychologists provide assessment of, and counseling for, personal, career, and educational problems. Counseling psychologists often use research to evaluate the effectiveness of treatments and to search for novel approaches to assessing problems and changing behavior. Research methods may include structured tests, interviews, interest inventories, and observations. Many work in academic

---

5. Many of the descriptions here are adapted with permission from *Careers in Psychology* (1986), a publication of the APA (see Resources).

settings, health care institutions, community mental health centers, hospitals, or private clinics.

Industrial/Organizational Psychology

Industrial/organizational psychologists are concerned with the relation between people and work. Their interests include organizational structure and organizational change; workers' productivity and job satisfaction; consumer behavior; selection, placement, training, and development of personnel; and the interaction between humans and machines. Their responsibilities on the job include research, development (translating the results of research into usable products or procedures), and problem solving.

Industrial/organizational psychologists work in businesses, industries, governments, and colleges and universities. Some may be self-employed as consultants or work for management consulting firms. In a business, industry, or government setting, industrial/organizational psychologists might study the procedures on an assembly line and suggest changes to reduce the monotony and increase the responsibility of workers. Or they might advise management on how to develop programs to identify staff with management potential or administer a counseling service for employees on career development and preparation for retirement.

School Psychology

School psychologists help educators and others promote the intellectual, social, and emotional development of children. They are also involved in creating environments that facilitate learning and mental health. They may evaluate and plan programs for children with special needs or deal with less severe problems such as disruptive behavior in the classroom. They sometimes engage in program development and staff consultation to prevent problems. They may also provide on-the-job training for teachers in classroom management, consult with parents and teachers on ways to support a child's efforts in school, and consult with school administrators on a variety of psychological and educational issues. School psychologists may be found in academic settings, where they train other school psychologists and do research. Other settings in which school psychologists work are nursery schools, day-care centers, hospitals, mental health clinics, private practice, federal and state government agencies, child guidance centers, penal institutions, and behavioral research laboratories.

Cognitive Psychology and Psycholinguistics

Cognitive and psycholinguistic psychologists are research-oriented psychologists with a focus of study comprising a number of characteristics. First, they study the behavior of knowing, as opposed to responding. They are concerned with finding scientific means for studying the mental processes involved in the acquisition and application of knowledge. Second, they emphasize the study of mental structure and organization. Finally, these psychologists view the individual as an active, constructive, and planful, rather than passive, recipient of environmental stimulation. Study of this area arose from the areas of linguistics and computer simulation: An information-processing theory evolved that resulted in a framework whereby human thought (cognition) and human language (linguistics) can be studied, analyzed, and understood. These researchers are most often found in academic research laboratory work or in advanced technological information-processing systems agencies.

Community Psychology

Community psychologists are concerned with everyday behavior in natural settings: the home, the neighborhood, and the workplace. They seek to understand the factors that contribute to normal and abnormal behavior in these settings. They also work to promote health and prevent disorder. Whereas clinical psychologists tend to focus on individuals who show signs of disorder, most community psychologists concentrate their efforts on groups of people who are not mentally ill (but may be at risk of becoming so) or on the population in general.

Developmental Psychology

Developmental psychologists study human development across the life span, from newborns to the aged. Developmental psychologists are interested in the description, measurement, and explanation of age-related changes in behavior; stages of emotional development; universal traits and individual differences; and abnormal changes in development. Observational as well as experimental methods are used to investigate such areas as aging, basic learning processes, cognition, perception, language acquisition, socialization, and sex roles. Many doctoral-level developmental psychologists are employed in academic settings: teaching and doing research. Others are employed by public school systems, hospitals, and clinics. They often consult on programs in day-care centers, preschools, and hospitals and clinics for children. They also evaluate intervention programs designed by private, state, or federal agencies.

Educational Psychology

Educational psychologists study how people learn, and they design the methods and materials used to educate people of all ages. Many educational psychologists work in universities, in both psychology departments and schools of education. Their research focuses on the theory and development of psychological tests, creativity, and retardation, as well as on such concepts as maturation, group behavior, curriculum development, and intellectual growth and development. They conduct basic research on topics related to the learning of reading, writing, mathematics, and science. Some educational psychologists develop new methods of instruction, including designing computer software. Others train teachers and investigate factors that affect teachers' performance and morale. Educational psychologists conduct research in schools and in federal, state, and local education agencies. They may be employed by governmental agencies or the corporate sector to analyze employees' skills and to design and implement training programs.

Engineering Psychology

Engineering psychologists promote the research, development, application, and evaluation of psychological principles relating human behavior to the characteristics, design, and use of environments and systems within which people work and live. They may be found working in industry where machine and computer design is required, in military and transportation facilities, or in city or architectural planning, for example.

Environmental Psychology

Environmental psychologists investigate the interrelationship between people and their sociophysical milleu. They study the effects on behavior of physical factors such as pollution and crowding and of sociophysical settings such as hospitals, parks, housing developments, and work environments, as well as the effects of behavior on the environment. These environments range from homes and offices to urban areas. Environmental psychologists may do basic research, for example, on people's attitudes toward different environments or their sense of personal space, or their research may be applied, such as evaluating an office design or assessing the psychological impact of a government's plan to build a new waste-treatment site.

Experimental Psychology

"Experimental psychologist" is a general title applied to a diverse group of psychologists who conduct research and often teach about a variety of basic behavioral processes. These processes include learning; sensation; perception; human performance; motivation; memory; language, thinking, and communication; and the physiological processes underlying behaviors such as eating, reading, and problem solving. Experimental psychologists study the basic processes by which humans take in, store, retrieve, express, and apply knowledge. They also study the behavior of animals, often with a view to gaining a better understanding of human behavior, but sometimes also because it is intrinsically interesting. Most experimental psychologists work in academic settings, teaching courses and supervising students' research in addition to conducting their own research. Experimental psychologists are also employed by research institutions, business, industry, and government.

Health Psychology

Health psychologists are researchers and practitioners concerned with psychology's contribution to the promotion and maintenance of good health and the prevention and the treatment of illness. As applied psychologists or clinicians, they may, for example, design and conduct programs to help individuals stop smoking, lose weight, manage stress, prevent cavities, or stay physically fit. As researchers, they seek to identify conditions and practices that are associated with health and illness. For example, they might study the effects of relocation on an elderly person's physical well-being. In public service roles, they study and work to improve the government's policies and systems for health care. Employment settings for this specialty area can be found in medical centers, industry, hospitals, health maintenance organizations, rehabilitation centers, public health agencies, and private practice.

Neuropsychology and Psychobiology

Psychobiologists and neuropsychologists investigate the relation between physical systems and behavior. Topics they study include the relation of specific biochemical mechanisms in the brain to behavior, the relation of brain structure to function, and the chemical and physical changes that occur in the body when we experience different emotions. Neuropsychologists also diagnose and treat disorders related to the central nervous system. They may diagnose behavioral disturbances related to suspected dysfunctions of the central nervous system and treat patients by teaching them new ways to acquire and process information—a technique known as cognitive retraining.

Clinical neuropsychologists work in the neurology, neurosurgery, psychiatric, and pediatric units of hospitals, and in clinics. They also work in academic settings, where they conduct research and train other neuropsychologists, clinical psychologists, and medical doctors.

Psychology of Aging (Geropsychology)

Researchers in the psychology of aging (geropsychology) draw on sociology, biology, and other disciplines as well as psychology to study the factors associated with adult development and aging. For example, they may investigate how the brain and the nervous system change as humans age and what effects those changes have on behavior or how a person's style of coping with problems varies with age. Clinicians in geropsychology apply their knowledge about the aging process to improve the psychological welfare of the elderly. Many people interested in the psychology of aging are trained in a more traditional graduate program in psychology, such as experimental, clinical, developmental, or social psychology. Although they are enrolled in such a program, they become geropsychologists by focusing their research, course work and practical experiences on adult development and aging. Geropsychologists are finding jobs in academic settings, research centers, industry, health care organizations, mental health clinics, and agencies serving the elderly. Some are engaged in private practice, either as clinical or counseling psychologists or as consultants on such matters as the design and evaluation of programs.

Psychometrics/Quantitative Methods

Psychometric and quantitative psychologists are concerned with the methods and techniques used in acquiring and applying psychological knowledge. A psychometrician may revise old intelligence, personality, and aptitude tests or devise new ones. These tests might be used in clinical, counseling, and school settings, or in business and industry. Other quantitative psychologists might assist a researcher in psychology or in another field in designing or interpreting the results of an experiment. To accomplish these tasks, they may design new techniques for analyzing information. Psychologists specializing in this area are generally well-trained in mathematics, statistics, and computer programming and technology.

Social Psychology

Social psychologists study how people interact with each other and how they are affected by their social environments. They study individuals as well as groups, observable behaviors, and private thoughts. Topics of interest to social psychologists include personality theories, the formation of attitudes and attitude change, attractions between people such as friendship and love, prejudice, group dynamics, and violence and aggression. Social psychologists might, for example, study how attitudes toward the elderly influence the elderly person's self-concept, or they might investigate how unwritten rules of behavior develop in groups and how those rules regulate the conduct of group members. Social psychologists can be found in a wide variety of academic settings, as well as in advertising, corporations, hospitals, educational institutions, and architectural and engineering firms as researchers, consultants, and personnel managers.

This limited sample of areas in psychology is intended to give you a general idea of the scope and variety of options available to you. You can also get information about particular concentrations by becoming familiar with APA divisions, many of which have career and training contacts (see Appendix B; some divisions have printed career descriptions as well—see Resources) and by perusing the various journals in psychology (also see Resources). You are also encouraged to explore the areas of study that interest you in greater depth by talking to faculty, students, and practitioners involved in those areas. First, read in the areas that interest you most and then consider contacting one or more people in those fields. It may feel intimidating at first to call a person whose work you have read about, but most psychologists are open to focused inquiries by students who have done their homework (more on this in chapter 5).

Choosing a Degree

The crucial consideration when choosing a degree is whether that degree represents the credentials you will need for employment in your field. What a degree allows you to do is far more important than a particular degree designation. Once you narrow your focus to one or two areas that interest you, it will not be difficult to discover what kinds of training and which degree to seek. As an exercise, read employment ads for psychologists in general newspapers, in the *APA Monitor* (the official newspaper of the APA), and in professional journals. This will give you a good idea of the kinds of credentials being sought by employers in specific areas.

The Doctoral Degree

The doctoral degree is recognized by the APA as the basic credential for psychologists and the entry-level degree to the profession. As mentioned before, many jobs, as well as licenses to practice, require a doctorate. At the doctoral level, your three basic options (in order of prevalence) are doctor of philosophy (PhD), doctor of psychology (PsyD), and doctor of education (EdD). Which degree is awarded by a program is generally a reflection both of the training model and of the institutional setting in which a program is housed. The PhD, then, is usually the degree granted by university-based psychology departments that train in the research or scientist–practitioner models, although some professional programs award the PhD as well. The PsyD is usually granted by a university-based or freestanding professional school of psychology that trains with the professional model. The EdD is a psychology PhD that is granted by a university-based education department, as opposed to a psychology department, and, like the PhD, usually reflects either the research or the scientist–practitioner training model.

The Master's Degree

Although the doctorate is required to be called a psychologist, at the same time a number of stimulating jobs and career opportunities involving psychological expertise are open to graduates with a master's degree in psychology. There are four permutations of master's degrees in the field: master of arts (MA), master of science (MS), and a terminal or nonterminal master's. There is very little difference between an MA and an MS degree in psychology. Most typically, the acronym reflects the department or school in which the program is housed. Like that of doctoral programs, the orientation of master's programs can be more or less practice or research based. More significant than the distinction between the MA and MS is the distinction between a master's and a master's-only degree (or "terminal" master's degree). Terminal programs are those intended to prepare you for a specific occupation that requires only a master's degree for entry-level employment. The nonterminal master's degree is awarded to students as part of their doctoral degree program.

If you decide to apply to master's programs and have any intention of pursuing a doctoral psychology degree after earning your master's, you may not want to apply to a program offering only a terminal master's degree. You should be aware that transfers from a terminal master's program to a doctoral program within the same school may not be permitted. If you do get a terminal master's degree and then apply to a doctoral program in another institution, none, or very few, of your master's-level credits may be applied toward your doctoral degree. As we mentioned earlier, the nonterminal master's degree is awarded to doctoral students on their way to earning a PhD, almost always in the same program. To earn this type of master's degree, you must apply to the doctoral program at the outset.

There are other disadvantages, as well as some advantages, to choosing a master's degree over a PhD, PsyD, or EdD. Let's start with the advantages. Admission requirements, particularly for GPAs and standardized test scores, are a little less stringent for master's applicants than for doctoral applicants. A master's degree also takes less time to earn (2–4 years compared with 4–7 years for a doctoral degree), so the cost is significantly less. Some, but not all, master's programs allow part-time study (some PsyD programs do as well, however). Most important, a master's degree provides sufficient training and credentials for a large number of employment arenas; there are many career opportunities for master's degree holders, particularly in nonclinical areas.

The master's option, then, may seem less daunting because it will require a smaller investment of time and money. It may also afford the flexibility of part-time study (a rarity in doctoral programs) and may provide a testing ground (albeit an expensive one) if you are not completely sure that a doctorate in psychology is the degree for you.

But there are disadvantages in some situations. For example, career options for master's degree holders are limited by state licensing and certification regulations. In the majority of states, master's degree holders cannot obtain a license that would qualify them for independent practice.

Furthermore, as mentioned before, only doctoral-level psychologists can hold the title "psychologist." Master's-level graduates generally earn less than do doctoral-level graduates, and the salary ceiling is lower. Furthermore, full membership in the APA and in many state psychological associations is restricted for master's degree holders. Those who meet certain criteria can attain full membership in the District of Columbia Psychological Association and in 14 of the 50 state associations, associate membership in 31 state associations, and affiliate membership in 3 state associations; 2 state associations have no membership category for master's degree holders. Full membership status confers the right to vote and hold office; therefore, master's degree holders are not universally permitted to participate in policy making related to their field.

You must decide if the advantages of a master's degree outweigh the disadvantages in your particular case. If you choose to go the master's route and are not sure you intend to apply to doctoral programs upon completion of a master's degree, your task in choosing programs will be somewhat more complex. As mentioned earlier, some doctoral programs do not credit hours earned in a terminal master's program, and those that do usually have specific requirements that may require you to retake some coursework. So take great care in selecting a master's program if a doctoral degree is your ultimate goal. While you are working on your master's degree, there are several things you can do to increase your attractiveness as a doctoral applicant:

- Get as much research experience as possible;
- establish good relationships with professors, who can later support your doctoral ambitions;
- get the broadest training possible, and get a good foundation in core subjects;
- maintain good grades; and
- obtain practica experiences in the areas on which you wish to concentrate.

What You Should Know About Accreditation, Licensure, and Certification

Generally speaking, accreditation of educational entities (programs or schools) is an assurance made by a formally recognized agency that the entity meets that agency's standards for quality. In the case of psychology, the APA is the major agency empowered to set standards for and evaluate graduate programs.[6] Before you zero in on your program choices, you should consider how important accreditation status is to your particular career goals. Here are some basic facts about APA accreditation to help you weigh your decision.

- The APA accredits only programs in three specialty areas—clinical, counseling, and school psychology—and only programs that train in the scientist–practitioner and professional models across these specialties.
- The APA accredits at the program level, not the school level; therefore, it is possible for two programs within the same school to have different accreditation status (e.g., the counseling program may be accredited whereas the clinical program may not).
- There are three levels of APA accreditation: (a) full, (b) provisional (conferred on programs that do not currently meet all criteria but appear to be able to do so in the near future), and (c) probation (conferred on programs that previously met criteria but appear not to be complying presently).
- Programs are evaluated regularly for accreditation by the APA, and status can change from one year to the next.
- APA accreditation is a voluntary process whereby each program may or may not request accreditation.
- There are training sites and employers that either prefer or require that their employees train in or graduate from APA-accredited programs.
- Competition for admission to APA-accredited programs is higher than for nonaccredited programs.
- Whereas you can be fairly certain that APA-accredited programs meet high standards of quality, lack of such accreditation does not necessarily mean the opposite. There are excellent programs that simply have not yet requested evaluation or are too new to be eligible.

How does accreditation differ from certification and licensure? In brief, accreditation is conferred on programs and institutions. Certification and licensure are conferred on individuals. Certification laws primarily regulate the use of the title "psychologist." Licensure laws regulate

---

6. Regional accreditation of institutions is also important (e.g., in transferring course credits). All programs listed in *Grad Study* are from institutions that are regionally accredited.

use of the title as well, but their primary aim is to regulate the mode and manner in which professionals using the title "psychologist" provide their services to the public. If you aspire to practice psychology independently and without supervision, as many clinical and counseling psychologists do, you will need a license. To obtain a license, you must pass a state board exam (oral, written, or both). Most states require you to hold a doctoral degree and to have completed 2 years of supervised practice to qualify for the exam. Each state has its own regulations for licensure and certification, however.

Accreditation status and licensure may be crucial issues for you if you aspire to be a practitioner and may not be relevant at all if you desire only to teach or to do research. *Grad Study* contains detailed explanations of accreditation and licensing, so you may want to read that account as well. Before applying to a graduate program, any student planning to seek licensure should contact the examining board for psychologists in the state where he or she intends to practice (if you're not sure where you will end up, contact the board in the state you currently live or in the states of the programs you are considering). We have included the addresses and phone numbers of such boards in each state in Appendix C. From these boards, you can inquire about the requirements for practice in that state and the status of the institutions offering the graduate programs you are considering.

Conclusion

In this chapter, we have attempted to provide a broad picture of the field of psychology today, the models of training, and the types of graduate degrees that are offered. We have raised several issues, such as accreditation, certification, and licensure, that are pertinent to decisions about pursuing graduate study in psychology, particularly for those interested in clinical, counseling, and school psychology.

In chapter 4, we return to the subject of your qualifications, going into more detail about what psychology programs are looking for and what you can do to improve your chances for acceptance. Finding the correct "fit" between you and the programs to which you apply is a repetitive process of looking within (at your interests, qualifications, and career goals) and looking out (at program emphases, requirements, and degrees), over and over again. By being realistic about both at this stage of the process, you are likely to maximize the chances of a good fit while minimizing the likelihood of a painful pinch as you plan your career.

Assessing Your Qualifications and Improving Your Chances for Acceptance

What we must decide is perhaps how we are valuable, rather than how valuable we are.—*F. Scott Fitzgerald*

In this chapter, we return to the topic of what graduate schools are looking for in their applicants. At the outset, we'd like you to be aware that, despite the commonalities we discuss in this chapter, every program is unique and will weigh admission requirements differently. Some are quite stringent about previous coursework in psychology, GPAs, and standardized test scores, whereas others will be more flexible and will look for other qualifications that might indicate strong promise in an applicant and that might increase the diversity of their applicant pool. Each program will also weigh less "objective" criteria differently. For example, some will emphasize letters of recommendation; others will focus more on personal essays and interview performance. Most admissions committees, however, will look at the total package of applicant qualifications in the context of the program's current goals.

In view of this, we urge you not to get too discouraged if you discover that you are not optimally qualified according to one specific criterion, such as GRE scores. Few students are perfectly qualified according to the criteria we discuss, yet many are accepted in the programs of their choice. Some programs may judge that your strengths in some areas compensate for shortcomings in others. For example, if you have significant and successful research experience in psychology, this may help offset relatively low test scores.

As we look at standards for each of these criteria in this chapter, we will also look at ways you can enhance your qualifications to improve your chances for acceptance. Sometimes this will involve intense preparation (e.g., for taking the GREs); other times, it will involve strategizing (e.g., lining up the right people to write letters of recommendation). In

---

Exhibit 4.1

Evaluation Criteria Used by Selection Committees

Objective Criteria

- GPA (overall GPA, psychology GPA, and last-2-years GPA)
- Standardized test scores (GRE-V, GRE-Q, GRE-Analytical, and GRE-Psychology; MAT)
- Coursework (number of hours, subject area, and level)

Nonobjective Criteria

- Letters of recommendation
- Experience
  - Research experience
  - (Field-related) work experience
  - Clinically related public service
- Application essays
- Interview performance
- Extracurricular activities

Unspecified Criteria

- Resume
- Quality of application materials
- School and work-site attitudes and behavior
- Special projects and honors courses
- Diversity

---

chapter 6, you will take steps to present your qualifications to admissions committees. The purpose of this chapter is to get you thinking about what you can do (or can plan to do) to improve those qualifications now.

What Are Graduate Psychology Programs Looking For?

As we discussed in chapter 2, graduate programs use a variety of criteria to evaluate the qualifications of applicants. These evaluation criteria tend to fall into two categories: objective and nonobjective. Look at the program entries in *Grad Study*. You will see three headings under Admission Requirements: Courses, Minimum Scores/GPAs, and Other Criteria. Coursework, scores, and GPAs fall into the category of objective criteria because these are all easily quantifiable measures of academic performance. "Other criteria" refers to a range of nonobjective criteria, such as letters of recommendation, application essays, interview performance, experience, and extracurricular activities, that are used by programs to further evaluate candidates, especially to differentiate between candidates whose objective academic qualifications are similar or to make special considerations when there is a disparity between objective measures (e.g., high GPA but low test scores).

Exhibit 4.1 lists all of the evaluation criteria used by selection committees and their approximate order of importance. In addition to objective and nonobjective criteria, we have included a category of "unspecified" criteria, so named because programs rarely specify these aspects, but they can be indirectly influential when it comes to choosing between otherwise equally qualified candidates. Programs listed in *Grad Study* state minimum coursework, GPAs, and standardized test scores as being required (R) or preferred (P) for admission, and they designate the importance of nonobjective criteria as being low, medium, or high. Table 4.1 shows the relative importance assigned by many programs to the six most commonly cited nonobjective criteria, as listed in *Grad Study*.

Because specific admission requirements vary so much among programs and because there are so many criteria used, it is impossible to state a foolproof formula for success. We can, however, state one generalization about how programs prioritize admission requirements. Generally, programs look first for applicants who show some strength in at least one out of the four following categories: GPA, test scores, coursework, and letters of recommendation. Chances for further consideration and admission tend to increase for applicants who excel in two, three, or all four categories.

Other criteria usually come into play if an applicant passes muster for one or more of these first four criteria. It is not impossible for an applicant whose grades, coursework, test scores, and letters of recommendation are uniformly unremarkable to be accepted into a program, but it is highly unlikely, especially for highly competitive programs. In the remainder of the chapter, we will examine these criteria individually; keep in mind, however, that selection committees generally do not evaluate individual criteria in isolation from each other, but rather try to view each applicant's qualifications as a whole.

Objective Evaluation Criteria

GPA

Because they are a concrete index of your academic performance, grades serve a highly practical purpose for selection committees. They are in

Table 4.1

Importance Ratings Assigned by Doctoral Psychology Programs (by Percentage) to the Six Most Commonly Used Nonobjective Evaluation Criteria

Importance	Letters of recommen- dation	Research experience	Interview	Field- related work experience	Clinically related public service	Extra- curricular activity
None	1.5	2.0	27.5	7.0	14.5	18.5
Low	3.5	13.5	8.0	19.0	13.5	51.5
Medium	22.0	29.5	20.5	48.0	51.5	24.0
High	73.0	55.0	44.0	26.0	20.5	6.0

Note. This table was compiled by the Education Directorate of the American Psychological Association, using information reported by 200 department chairpersons who contributed to the 1992 edition of *Graduate Study in Psychology.*

effect a sample of how you are likely to perform in graduate school classes. You may demonstrate terrific potential as a clinician or incredible creativity when it comes to research design, but if you can't pass core graduate courses, you will not be able to earn your degree.

By averaging the minimum GPA requirements for doctoral programs listed in *Grad Study*, we have ascertained that the average minimum GPA that most programs look for is 3.2 (GPAs for master's programs are usually somewhat lower, e.g., 3.0). As we explained in chapter 2 (see "Admission Standards and Competition"), however, the way in which GPAs are rated varies from program to program. Some will have lower or higher required GPAs, others will look more closely at the last two years' GPA, and still others will also look at the GPA you received in psychology courses. As you will do in chapter 5, you need to consult individual programs in *Grad Study* to determine the required and preferred minimums and to discover whether a program weighs more heavily GPAs in general, GPAs for psychology, or GPAs for the last 2 years. Program committees are also aware that a certain GPA is more difficult to obtain at some schools than at others.

Although it is difficult to *significantly* raise the overall numerical value of a GPA, there are strategies you can use to improve your GPA standing. If you are a second- or third-year undergraduate, you can probably elevate your GPA a few decimal points if you obtain As in your remaining courses. If you are at that stage and have a GPA lower than the criteria for programs you are interested in (see chapter 5), we recommend that you consult with advisors and teachers and let them know that you are committed to improving your academic record. More than likely, they can help you by recommending tutors, referring you to study skills workshops or study groups, or in general guiding you toward better mastery of the subject matter of a particular course. As we mentioned, many programs do give more weight to your performance in the second half of your undergraduate training. Even if you have blots on your record for your first two years (e.g., poor grades in important courses, withdrawals, and incompletes), many selection committees will still look on you favorably if you demonstrate significant improvement in the latter part of your training.

If you are in your senior year or have completed your undergraduate training, improving your GPA standing will of course be more difficult, but it is not impossible for you to improve the impression your grades make. There are several strategies for you to consider. If you have just become a senior, one option is to earn As in additional courses (particularly those "preferred" by your choice programs) or retake courses for which you earned less than a B, although this may mean delaying graduation by a semester or two. (Be aware that earlier grades will remain on your transcript. However, if you do well the second time around, you will have demonstrated an improved academic potential as well as a commitment to your goal of attending graduate school.)

If you have already graduated and have taken all of the required courses for the programs you are most interested in, but are unhappy with your GPA, you may be able to demonstrate that your academic potential is higher than your undergraduate GPA indicates by taking one or two graduate psychology courses through the continuing education program at your local university. This will not only give admissions committees an updated sample of your academic performance, it will give you a taste of what graduate school will be like.

If you decide that taking additional courses, at either the graduate or the undergraduate level, is worthwhile, consider two pieces of advice. First, take only as much coursework as you can handle well. Neither your GPA nor your academic reputation will be enhanced if you cannot improve on your previous performance. Second, focus on courses that are regarded highly by graduate programs (see our discussion of undergraduate coursework later in this chapter; similar principles apply to taking graduate courses). For example, getting As in rigorous psychology courses (such as statistics and experimental psychology) may make more of an impression than the same grades in abnormal psychology or theories of personality, for example.

If taking additional coursework will not significantly improve your GPA, you may want to focus your efforts on preparing for the GREs and the MAT. As described below, many programs use GPAs in conjunction with test scores as an initial screening criterion. There is evidence to suggest, for example, that high GRE scores can offset mediocre GPAs. (However, lackluster GRE scores may reinforce the negative impression low GPAs may make.) Another strategy you can consider is to simply target graduate programs that place less priority on GPAs or have less competitive admission standards in that regard (see chapter 5). Be sure that your standing on other criteria, such as your letters of recommendation and personal essays, is superior (these are discussed later in this chapter and in chapter 6).

In general, the greater the competition for admission to a particular program, the more relevant your GPA will be. If your GPA just meets the minimum and you are competing with applicants whose GPAs exceed the minimum, you will need to excel in other respects to remain competitive. Probably the best strategy for ameliorating the effect of mediocre grades, then, is to compensate with excellent qualifications in as many other areas as possible. As we have suggested, obtaining high GRE scores, taking rigorous courses, carefully writing and rewriting your personal essays, and garnering solid letters of recommendation are especially recommended.

Standardized Test Scores

Most graduate programs in psychology use scores on the general GRE and Psychology GRE as admission criteria, and a much smaller number use scores from the Miller Analogies Test (MAT). International students may have to take an additional test, the Test of English as a Foreign Language (TOEFL; see Resources). Regular test dates for the GREs are in October, December, February, April, and June, but by paying a higher fee, you can now take the computerized general GRE (but not the Psychology GRE) any week of the year (see footnote on p. 5, and also see Resources). Test dates for the MAT vary, depending on the test site. You should take the MAT *no later* than 8 weeks prior to your earliest application deadline and the GREs no later than 6 weeks prior (or 2–3 weeks prior if you are taking the computerized general GRE at a Sylvan Learning Center). The longer the lead time, the more opportunities you will have to actively study for the tests, which we recommend. If you are planning early, you may even want to take the exams several months earlier (e.g., in June) to allow for the possibility of retaking them.

To take the Psychology GRE or the paper-and-pencil version of the general GRE, you must apply at least 5 weeks in advance of the testing date (4 weeks if you are willing to pay a late registration fee). If you are reading this chapter in August or early September and want to take the GREs in October, you should apply immediately, before reading any further. If it is any later than that, you should call the 800 number in the Resources and arrange for computerized testing. If you are a student with a disability who will need special services to take the exams, you should apply at least several weeks in advance of the regular application deadline (see test bulletins for exact dates and detailed instructions). Because the MAT has no nationally scheduled test administration dates, you must consult the *List of Testing Centers*, available from the Psychological Corporation (see Resources) and in many undergraduate counseling centers and graduate admissions offices. Then you must call or write the institution hosting the MAT that is nearest to you. They will tell you when the next tests are scheduled to be administered.

What are these tests like? The general GRE consists of three components, each with a multiple-choice format. The Verbal Abilities (GRE-V) component contains analogy, antonym, sentence completion, and reading comprehension questions and exercises. Quantitative Abilities (GRE-Q) tests your ability to perform arithmetic, algebra, geometry, and quantitative comparisons and to interpret data. The GRE-V and GRE-Q are the two components most frequently used. The Analytical Abilities component, which is newer and less frequently used, contains analytical reasoning exercises and logic problems. Both individual and combined scores are generated; programs may require one or both. Each component yields a maximum score of 800; the average minimum score required for serious consideration for a doctoral program is 550 for any one component and 1200 for the combined GRE-V + GRE-Q. For master's programs, the average scores are a bit lower.

The Psychology GRE consists of about 220 questions drawn from a range of subject areas in psychology that cut across three categories: experimental or natural science (e.g., learning, cognition, perception, sensation, ethology, and comparative and physiological psychology), social science (e.g., personality, social, clinical, developmental, and abnormal psychology), and general psychology (e.g., history and systems, applied psychology, tests and measurement, and statistics). In addition to a total score for questions in all categories, two subscores are reported, although most programs use only the total score. As with the other test components, for doctoral programs, the average minimum score required for the Psychology GRE is 550. However, few schools will rule you out for lower scores on this test, if your other credentials are superior.

The MAT is a 50-minute, 100-item, analogy completion test that is quite different from the GREs. Because so few programs use the MAT and because required and preferred scores are sometimes not given, we can only give a general estimate of this criterion, which we calculate to be in the range of 60–70 correct answers. It will probably be the case that few, if any, of the programs you will target will require the MAT (those that do will usually also require the GREs). Check *Grad Study* carefully to determine whether you will need to take this test. If you do, follow the same kind of advice we give for preparing for the GREs.

How important are standardized test scores relative to other factors?

Again, we can only generalize. Because all programs use GPAs but not all programs use test scores to evaluate applicants, it is safe to say that, overall, test scores are slightly less important than GPAs. Also, some believe that standardized tests give a culturally biased picture of student potential, particularly for members of ethnic minorities, and so may weigh them less heavily than other criteria. As is the case with GPAs, however, test scores become more relevant as competition for admission increases: Many programs use test scores in conjunction with GPAs as an initial screening criterion, and this can be to your advantage if you have a good standing in both.

What can you do to ensure the best scores possible? Preparation is the key. Those who have prepared for many hours over several weeks or months believe that this preparation was a major factor in obtaining outstanding GRE and MAT scores. Forty to sixty hours of preparation is not overkill (just taking a practice test takes several hours). But the actual amount of time needed to prepare depends on the individual and his or her background and test-taking facility. In the beginning, take a couple of practice tests and see how well you do. The more you need to improve your scores, the more time you should spend reviewing.

We recommend that you obtain at least one of the many study guides available for the GREs and the MAT (see Resources) and that in addition to studying, you take a practice test at least once weekly several months in advance of the exam. (If you have only a few weeks left to prepare, take practice tests more frequently.) These guides will not only familiarize you with the mechanics of test taking, they will also help you identify skills or subject areas that you are weak or rusty in. This is particularly important for returning students who have been out of school for a while. Say, for example, that it has been many years since you studied algebra or geometry. Recognizing this, you should spend extra time on material in the test preparation books in these areas, and you may want to buy or borrow some math textbooks to use to review. International students may need to plan additional time for the verbal portions of tests, such as the GRE-Verbal, GRE-Psychology, GRE-Analytical, and MAT.

If you study, each week you should see some small improvement in your scores. Moreover, each time you take a practice test, you prime yourself favorably for the day of the actual exam. If you are sufficiently familiar with the test format, you will not have to waste time on the exam day reading and interpreting instructions but can instead focus on the content of the questions.

Finally, if you are the type of person who prepares more easily with external structure, you may want to take one of the preparation courses offered by businesses such as Kaplan's and the Princeton Review, which often advertise in college newspapers. The career preparation office at your local university may be able to direct you to such classes, and you might also be able to find them listed in the yellow pages of your phone book under "Schools." Returning students who have not taken exams in the classroom for years may find these courses particularly helpful.

Timing and preparation for the GRE-Subject (Psychology) test are somewhat different than for the general tests. First, if you are still an undergraduate, you should plan to take the test as late in the game as possible, to ensure that you have completed most of your undergraduate psychology courses. That is, you probably shouldn't take this exam until October of your senior year (or December if the application deadlines of your targeted schools allow for this), even if this precludes the possibility of retaking the test. Second, you can study for this test in a more content-focused way than you can for the GRE-General. The psychology test asks fact-based questions (e.g., about names, specific theories, concepts, and data, and parts and functions of the brain and nervous system). Given the range of subject matter covered, probably the best study guides you can use are undergraduate psychology textbooks. Your introductory psychology textbook can give you the best overview, but textbooks from specific areas of psychology described earlier can also be useful in your review. You can use the test bulletin as an outline of the subject areas that you need to have knowledge of, and there are preparation books for this test as well (see Resources).

What can you do if your test scores are not as high as you would like? As we mentioned earlier, it is possible to retake tests. Before using this strategy, however, consider a few points. First, be aware that the GREs and the MAT have a high test–retest reliability; that is, people who take the test at one time tend to score much the same at another time. Second, keep in mind that new scores do not replace previous scores; all scores will be reported by the testing agency. If your new scores are not significantly higher than your previous scores, you run the risk of reinforcing the impression your first scores made.

A decision to retake tests should be based on two factors: (a) Your previous scores may have been negatively influenced by some rectifiable circumstance (e.g., illness, extreme anxiety, or lack of sleep; failure to prepare adequately), and (b) you believe that you can improve on your score by at least 15% by rectifying those circumstances. For example, if on your practice exams you consistently scored over 15% higher than you did on the actual exam, but you had the flu the day you took the exam, you might reasonably consider retaking the exam. Also, if you did not prepare for the exam beforehand, you may be able to raise your score by quite a few points by consistent and thorough preparation before the next exam.

In any case, remember that test scores are usually considered in the context of your other qualifications. Therefore, if you are less than pleased with your scores, your GPA may compensate, and you can work hard on improving your qualifications in as many other areas as possible.

Coursework

You might think that graduate programs prefer candidates who have taken a large number of psychology courses or who have taken a concentration of courses in a particular area of psychology. In reality, many graduate psychology programs are more interested in generalists than specialists. The reason for this is that graduate programs are considered to be the appropriate place to specialize; a broad undergraduate education is often considered to be the best possible preparation for pursuing a specialty in graduate school. Therefore, program faculty may be reviewing your transcript for evidence that you have received a broad and well-rounded education. This means that, ideally, in addition to psychology, your coursework should cover a range of disciplines including physical and biological sciences, math, English literature and composition, history, philosophy, sociology and anthropology, and foreign language. Increasingly, programs are strongly preferring (if not requiring) at least one course in computer science.

On the other hand, although all programs seek well-rounded generalists, individual programs vary a great deal when it comes to undergraduate psychology course requirements and preferences. Take a few moments to peruse the admission requirements for *Grad Study* program entries, and you will see what we mean. Some programs are extremely specific about the types of courses they require (e.g., introductory psychology, statistics, research methods, learning, and abnormal psychology); others only state the number of undergraduate hours required in psychology courses (e.g., at least 18 hours) without specifying particular courses. Still others prefer certain psychology courses but do not require them for admission.

Some program descriptions in *Grad Study* state only that you should have an "appropriate psychology background." This kind of description can be frustrating. Even if you are reading this early in your undergraduate career and you are majoring in psychology, how can you be sure to take all the "right" courses when so much variation and ambiguity exist? It is not as problematic as it may seem. If you follow the reasoning in the following paragraph, you can increase your chances of ending up with a solid background in psychology that will be esteemed by most graduate programs.

The purpose of stipulating undergraduate course requirements is to ensure that applicants have had a basic foundation in the content and methods of psychology. Specifically, programs are seeking proof that applicants have acquired fundamental knowledge of research methodology, of the theoretical bases of psychology, and of the traditional content areas of psychology. For the majority of programs, at least one course in statistics is essential for any prospective graduate student of psychology; additional and higher level courses in statistics are especially highly regarded. In addition to statistics, courses that are valuable for learning the scientific methods and theoretical bases of psychology include history and systems, experimental and physiological psychology, learning, motivation, perception, sensation, abnormal psychology, tests and measurement, and foundation courses in research methodology. Additional content areas valued by many programs are developmental psychology, personality, social psychology, and industrial psychology. Introductory psychology courses are valuable for giving you a broad overview of these content areas, but you would be well advised to take individual courses in many of these subjects. Laboratory-based natural or biological science courses taken from departments other than psychology can nicely complement your training in psychological methods and theory. And, again, a computer science course is now frequently required or recommended.

You should be aware that some programs do indicate a preference for coursework that is closely related to your intended area of concentration; you will need to consult individual programs to discover what their particular preferences are. To cite but one example, courses in tests and measurement are frequently specified as being preferred by clinical and school psychology programs, as well as by some industrial/organizational ones.

There are several other useful things to keep in mind when planning your coursework or assessing your own transcript. Programs do tend to be biased toward math and science, because these kinds of courses convey a certain willingness and ability on your part to engage in scientific pursuits. If you are planning your strategy before your senior year, or if you are a returning student and are planning to take a few courses to update your credentials, perhaps a good way to increase your attractiveness as a candidate is to take a math or science course in addition to the psychology courses you plan to take. Research experience is extremely highly regarded, so it would also be to your advantage to opt for laboratory-based courses to the extent possible or to take courses with professors who are currently engaged in research that you might be able to assist with. In general, take the highest level of course you are capable of and lean toward rigorous courses. Such choices send the message that you are a serious and committed scholar who welcomes a challenge.

Psychology, like all sciences, is constantly changing as new theories, methodologies, and data appear. If you are returning to school and were a psychology major many years ago, even if you have all the required coursework, the content of the courses you have taken may be out-of-date. Although you can't take all of your undergraduate psychology courses over, you might consider taking one laboratory-based course (e.g., perception, sensation, learning, motivation, or comparative psychology) and an additional course that may be preferred by the schools you're most interested in. This would serve two additional objectives. First, you will to some extent have updated your credentials; the A or B you earn in the course is clearly what you are capable of now, not 10 years ago. Second, and we'll have more to say about this later, returning students often have difficulty locating people to write letters of recommendation who have current knowledge of their academic abilities. By taking a couple of courses and becoming acquainted with the professors through class participation and (even better) becoming involved in research, you have two candidates who might be appropriate to write such letters.

If you are interested in graduate school in psychology but you majored in some other discipline, you may have to postpone graduate school until you can get the required psychology courses. This will depend on the programs you wish to attend. Some require five or six undergraduate psychology courses (e.g., introductory psychology, statistics, experimental psychology, a laboratory-based course [e.g., learning, perception, sensation, motivation, comparative psychology], abnormal psychology, personality, history and systems, tests and measurements, and research methods are common). Others will prefer such courses but may not require them. As you work through the steps in chapter 5, it will become more clear which programs appeal to you most and what their requirements are. If you are extremely interested in several programs that require certain courses, it may be worth your while to take undergraduate psychology courses for one or two semesters. Or, you may decide to apply only to programs that don't have such requirements.

In summary, the strategies you use to meet or exceed the criteria of undergraduate coursework will depend on your status as an applicant and on the programs you most want to attend. If you have not yet completed your undergraduate education, you may have time to evaluate your course plans and make needed changes. If you have completed your undergraduate degree and have the time, you may want to consider taking some additional courses to round out your transcript. If you are unable to do anything to enhance your transcript prior to applying to a program, you may choose only programs that require the courses that you have already taken. In this case, you might also try to discern what academic strengths you have that are not obvious on your transcript (e.g., perhaps you did not take any laboratory or research courses, which the program prefers, but you have significant on-the-job research experience through which you learned those skills). Take care to reveal those strengths elsewhere (e.g., in your personal essay and resume).

Nonobjective Criteria

Nonobjective criteria include letters of recommendation, experience (i.e., research and psychology-related public service), application essays, interview performance, and extracurricular activities. Each program weighs nonobjective criteria differently, so you will need to look at each program's entry under Admission Requirements/Other Criteria in *Grad Study* to find the weight that program gives to a particular criterion (e.g., high, medium, or low). This can help you decide what to emphasize in your application. For example, if research experience is rated high, you might want to focus your personal essay as much as possible on your research. In general, if you are lacking in one or two of the objective criteria described earlier, you can enhance your application by presenting yourself most advantageously on these nonobjective criteria.

Letters of Recommendation

You will need to obtain an average of three letters of recommendation in applying to most graduate programs. Some programs supply their own forms (see Appendix D for a sample generic form; please note, however, that this is not an official form and is not endorsed by the APA). Others simply request letters, but the kind of information desired is similar for most programs. Committees want to know how long and how well the recommender has known the applicant and in what capacity, whether the applicant's academic record is a good reflection of his or her ability, and how he or she would judge the applicant's potential for success in graduate school. Often respondents are asked to rate the applicant on a variety of academic and personal characteristics, using a numeric scale (e.g., ability to use laboratory tools and equipment, oral and written verbal skills, creativity, maturity, leadership, social skills, independence, etc.). The program may ask the recommender to rate the applicant's potential for performing research and providing psychological services. Also commonly included is an open-ended question that invites the respondent to speak freely about the applicant.

Letters of recommendation are often considered to be the most important nonobjective criterion; sometimes they are given equal weight with GPAs and test scores. Although sterling recommendations probably cannot fully compensate for an applicant's mediocre academic record, they can be very persuasive in conjunction with a fairly good academic record. In other words, if a selection committee had to select only one candidate out of two who both had similar academic records, the candidate with the "better" letters of recommendation would probably have an advantage.

We discuss procedures for procuring recommendation letters in chapter 6; here we want to focus on whom you should ask and why. The best sources for recommendations are those people who will have the most pertinent and favorable things to say about your academic abilities and potential as a psychologist. The ideal source, then, might be a psychology professor with whom you have studied or collaborated recently; from whom you have taken at least one, preferably more than one, upper-level or highly valued course; from whom you received an "A"; and who knows you well academically and, perhaps, personally. It is crucial that at least one of your letters be written by someone who meets as many of these criteria as possible. If you are unable to procure all of the letters required from among your psychology professors, good complementary sources include professors of math, science, or composition who could speak favorably of your proficiency with statistics, your orientation toward science, or your writing ability in particular and academic qualifications in general. People who supervised a research or field-related project or psychology-related work experience are potentially good sources, especially if they are trained psychologists or other mental health professionals, such as psychiatrists, clinical social workers, or licensed counselors. Avoid letters from friends, relatives, co-workers, and even supervisors on your job, unless that job is specifically psychology related. In general, opt for letters from academic sources over those from the business world, unless there is an important reason to include such sources (e.g., a plant superintendent knows of psychology-related work you have done that is directly relevant to the industrial/organizational program you are applying to).

Most returning students are likely to have lost touch with their former professors (unless it was an unusually close student–faculty relationship, professors from more than a few years ago cannot write an informed letter), and so this part of the application might be quite a challenge. Meeting potential sources through taking additional psychology, math, or science courses before applying to graduate school is one strategy that has been mentioned. If you choose this route, be sure to get into a class that is small enough for the professor to get to know you.

Another strategy is to find a psychologist at a local university who would allow you to assist with some of his or her research over a period of several months. This might require some homework before contacting this person, such as contacting a local psychology department and finding out the kind of research its faculty are involved in and then searching *PsycLIT* (a computerized database of publications in psychology, available at most university libraries). After you contact the psychologists whose work most interests you, you will need to be sure that you will work to some extent directly with them, and not solely with their graduate student research assistants. This can be a delicate negotiation that will be easier if you are sufficiently familiar with the researcher's work and can make a case for being directly involved with him or her. The benefits that could accrue from this relationship, however, extend way beyond the considerable boon regarding letters of recommendation. Becoming actively involved in someone else's research can help you define your own area of study. At the very least, it will give you a realistic idea of the complexity of psychological research and a respect for methodological rigor and statistical techniques. These two strategies—additional coursework and research—are even more important if your objective qualifications are not sterling. However, if your objective and other nonobjective qualifications are strong for the most part and if taking a course or getting involved in research is not an option for some reason, select recommenders in a respectable role (supervisors, for example, are better than peers at work) who can link their experiences with you as much as possible to your academic abilities and to your potential as a psychologist.

Be aware that not every letter needs to cover every aspect of your career potential and your academic skills. Your primary goal should be to ensure that all of the information requested by the program from recommenders is covered by the combination of your letters (see chapter 6 for more details). For now, your task is simply to consider whether you now know people who can provide the kind of letter needed or whether you need to factor in time for such people to become acquainted with you and your abilities.

Experience

In general, selection committees value research experience most highly, but they also view other psychology-related work experiences, paid or volunteer, positively. The fact that you took the initiative to gain practical experience shows that you had substantial interest in psychology in the first place. It also demonstrates that you made a conscious and early effort to associate yourself with the profession, find out more about it, and test the waters, so to speak, before deciding to pursue a graduate-level career. Applicants with significant psychology-related work experiences can often speak more knowledgeably about their career goals. So, if you have such experiences, make them visible—in your application, essay, letters of recommendation, and interview. (Returning students may have an advantage here, particularly if their years of work experience can be related to psychology or to the specific program to which they are applying.) If you don't have such experiences, you may still have time to get them. Even a brief mention on your application that you will be volunteering at a hospice during the spring of your senior year (if that is truly the case), for example, may enhance your application and also provide you with experience you can share if you are called for an interview.

Grad Study program entries list and rate the importance of three categories of experience under "other criteria": research experience, (field-related) work experience, and clinically related public service. Research experience usually relates to psychology, but might also include research in related fields such as sociology or biology. Field-related work experiences means psychology experience in general as well as in a particular concentration area. Clinically related public service includes the provision of most human services that are related to mental health. Insofar as evaluation criteria are concerned, programs do make distinctions among specific kinds of experiences and evaluate them differently, depending on the type of program and its particular training bent. For example, your experience on a hotline may be weighed more heavily by a clinical program than by an industrial/organizational one. However, research experience is considered by most programs as the most valuable type of experience to have, regardless of the training model (with the exception of some PsyD programs). These experiences are particularly valuable if they are supervised by a psychologist, but supervision by a psychiatrist, social worker, or other professional with social science or mental health credentials is also viewed positively.

How do you decide how much and what kind of experience to seek and to identify on your application? Quality is definitely more important than quantity. If you are applying to a research-oriented program, research experience will generally benefit your status as an applicant, whereas human services experience may not, relatively speaking. Although practice-oriented programs tend to place less emphasis on research experience, such experience is still highly valued. Furthermore, the experience criterion is probably more influential for clinical applicants simply because the competition for admission is greater.

As we emphasized in chapter 3, regardless of your bent toward research or practice, research will be an integral component of most graduate programs in psychology. Having successful research experience as a credential is probably the best way to demonstrate your promise as a scientist. Programs will often view research experience as a strong indication that you will be both willing and able to complete your thesis or dissertation.

The most common way to obtain research experience is to assist a psychology professor with his or her own research. More knowledgeable and motivated students can also design and conduct their own research projects through an independent study. There are two less common but viable alternatives. One is to assist in a research project with a professor in another department (e.g., biology, computer science, sociology). Another is to volunteer as a research assistant in a nonuniversity setting such as a hospital or mental health clinic. Independent study and volunteer research outside of the university are especially good options for applicants who do not currently have close ties to a university and do not have time to do undergraduate research or to take a course before applying to a graduate program.

In terms of field-related work, try to gain experience related to the area in which you want to concentrate. For clinical and counseling programs, work done in an established mental health or human services setting, under the direct supervision of a psychologist or other licensed mental health professional, is held in high esteem. For industrial/organizational programs, hands-on experience with personnel issues, training, and organizational change in business, government, or industry, for example, is highly valued. Experience working in the school system would be quite appropriate for those interested in educational or school psychology, as would experience in a preventive health care organization or rehabilitative medical center for those interested in health psychology. The main point is that you should tailor your field-related experiences to the type of program you want to attend. Experience that is considered an asset by one program may be seen as not applicable by another.

As with research experience, programs are likely to take you more seriously if you have already had some professional exposure to providing psychological services before applying to graduate school. More specifically, they look at field-related experience as an indication that you are personally fit for a career in clinical or applied psychology (e.g., you can apply psychological knowledge to help solve problems; you have the interpersonal skills to work with a variety of people, often under stress). Clinical and other applied programs are looking for some confirmation that you have the maturity and social skills that would enable you to be an effective practitioner or organizational member. Again, returning students who have demonstrated these qualities in their work histories may have an edge here.

For those interested in clinical and counseling programs, there are some opportunities for gaining part-time, paid experience in human service fields (e.g., as a psychiatric technician in an inpatient mental health facility), and volunteer opportunities are quite ample, especially in community agencies. A good way to begin your search for meaningful experience is to decide on a population or a work setting that interests you particularly, or to locate a professional psychologist whose work you are particularly interested in. Good resources to assist you in finding work include career counselors, psychology department advisers, mental health associations, and local government agencies (most counties have volunteer assistance programs of one kind or another). Some examples of work that you would be qualified to do before you enter graduate school include answering hotlines or providing information and referral services at campus or community counseling and crisis centers; working as a companion to children (e.g., Big Brother/Big Sister) or adults (e.g., nursing home residents); assisting juvenile delinquents or welfare families through social service agencies; working as a psychiatric aid at a hospital or clinic; or helping private or group practice clinicians compile results of question-naires or tests.

Those interested in industrial/organizational programs or human factors engineering, for example, may also find paid and volunteer op-portunities with the military, government, and private industry. These openings may be less visible than those in human services agencies, so you may have to do more research to find them. If you don't already know of organizations doing the kind of work you want to be trained to do, a good starting point might be the career counseling center of your local university. They are often aware of which companies or agencies will provide valuable experience in return for unpaid (and sometimes paid) labor. Another strategy is to peruse journals in the areas you want to practice and find the institutional affiliations of the authors. Although many of them will be university affiliated, a good number will work in an organizational setting that may have branches in your geographical area.

Equally important as seeking experience that is appropriate to your career orientation is making sure that you create a good impression on your supervisors. Whether you are being paid or not, you are expected to conduct yourself as a professional, which means being reliable (showing up for work, being on time, completing assigned tasks, etc.), being willing to assume responsibility appropriately, exhibiting interest in and enthu-siasm for your work, and so forth. Experience will not be a helpful cre-dential if you do not perform professionally.

Try to get as much value as you can from your work experiences, whatever they are. For example, if you are assisting on a research project, see if you can earn authorship credit, which is a very impressive credential. Establish a good rapport with your supervisors, show them what you're capable of, and earn their respect; these people can be valuable resources for you and may have the power to influence your application through letters of recommendation.

One final caution: Even the most valuable experience cannot fully compensate for a low GPA, particularly in your final two years of school. If you are trying to gain experience while you are still in school, make sure that your academic performance does not suffer as a result of work-ing.

Application Essays

Most programs will require you to write at least one essay for inclusion with your application, and these essays are taken quite seriously in evaluating applicants. For one thing, they may be the most revealing of you as a unique individual (i.e., they paint a more distinctive picture than do GPAs and GRE scores). For another, they are samples of your thought-fulness, writing ability, and appropriate creativity.

Programs refer to these essays by various names, but most commonly they are called personal essays, career goal statements, or statements of purpose. Occasionally, you will be asked for an autobiographical essay. You will usually be given guidelines on length and what kind of infor-mation to include. The three most typical themes targeted by these essays are your long-term career plans, your areas of interest in psychology, and your reasons for choosing a particular program. Unfortunately, each of the programs you're interested in may ask for a slightly different slant on one or more of these themes, so you must be prepared to tailor each essay to each program's requirements.

Program committees will be attending not only to what you have to say about yourself, but also how you say it. These essays can reveal a great deal about you, overtly or subtly. For example, they can reveal your opinion of yourself, your level of confidence, your values and priorities, and the general way in which you think and express yourself. Well-written, articulate essays can be very persuasive, and poorly thought-out and badly written essays can be very damaging. More details on writing such essays appear in chapter 6. For now, we'd like to impress on you the importance of allowing sufficient time to draft and rewrite essays, which includes not only the time you actually write, but also the time needed to let ideas germinate and to get feedback on your essays from others. If you get applications as early as possible, you will know ahead of time the kinds of essays you will be writing and you will have enough time to ponder your approach. You might also begin to line up people to review your essays as early as possible, because this is a time-consuming task.

Interview Performance

Many programs request interviews (commonly referred to as preselection interviews) with applicants some time between receiving applications and making final selections. If you are asked to appear for an interview, chances are that you are among the final pool of applicants being seriously considered for admission. Because of this, your interview performance will be of great importance. Although chronologically, interviews will be the last step you take in applying, it's useful to think about them now so that you can collect the information you'll need to prepare for them at the same time you are gathering information about programs (see chapter 5). Also, by thinking about the likelihood of such interviews now, you have time to budget the money for the trips you may have to take.

Preselection interviews are not unlike job interviews in several respects. One of the primary purposes of a job interview is to assess how well the applicant seems to fit into the organization. The same is true of preselection interviews: The interviewer will be interested foremost in assessing how well you seem to fit into the program you are applying to. Probably the most important thing you can do to prepare for an interview, then, is to thoroughly acquaint yourself with the program (e.g., determine its training model, areas of concentration, and philosophy; have some familiarity with faculty members and their particular areas of interest; etc.) and to be able to show how your interests and qualifications "fit" the program.

Interviews also make it possible for selection committees to assess a variety of personal characteristics (e.g., interpersonal skills, verbal expression, confidence, personality style, grooming, etc.). Specific faculty may also be viewing candidates with an eye to whether you might be interested in working in their particular areas of research. If you do your homework and are thoroughly familiar with your own application materials and the program you are applying to, and if you have taken some time to clarify your goals and your reasons for applying, it will be easier for you to relax and speak with some confidence in your interview. If you appear to be uncertain of your own goals and have not taken the trouble to thoroughly research the program, you are probably going to seem as if you lack focus, seriousness, or interest.

We will discuss interviews in depth in chapter 7. For now, plan time in your schedule to rehearse. It never hurts to role-play for an interview, and it can significantly reduce your anxiety during the actual interview. You'll want to devise a list of likely questions (sample questions are listed in chapter 7) and have a friend or colleague play the role of interviewer. Target those questions on which you seem to fumble, and keep rehearsing until your answers seem to come naturally.

Interviewers are looking for anything that makes you stand out in comparison with the other final applicants. Try to view the interview as an opportunity to emphasize your strengths and compensate for your weaknesses, and to bring forth any special talents or characteristics that make you uniquely qualified for enrollment.

Finally, perhaps the best advice we can give you in regard to interviews is, if you are invited, go! Declining an interview can be viewed very negatively and can be interpreted as a lack of interest. Those who do not attend can be at a disadvantage when compared with those who made good impressions on their interviews.

Extracurricular Activities

Extracurricular activities are those that are not directly related to your academic or work interests and experiences and that mainly involve participation in clubs and organizations. Although these may have been important in applying to undergraduate school, they are much less influential in graduate admissions. Those that are important are more limited in scope. Membership in organizations, for example, may only be pertinent if they are psychology-related organizations. Organizations you might consider include the American Psychological Association (some divisions offer student affiliate membership); regional, state, and specialty-area psychological associations; psychological associations geared to specific populations, such as women and ethnic minorities; Psi Chi or Psi Beta, the national honor societies for students of psychology; and other university-affiliated psychology students' groups. The American Psychological Association of Graduate Students also offers memberships to undergraduate students (for contact information on these organizations, see Resources).

Such organizational affiliation will be somewhat more influential if you were or are in a leadership position (e.g., being elected as an officer or a student representative; chairing a committee; etc.). However, although such activities can be perceived as an indication of your interest in and commitment to psychology, they have relatively weak power to offset important credentials such as grades and standardized test scores.

Indirectly, however, membership and participation in such organizations can have a significant impact on your candidacy. These organizations sponsor conventions, meetings, and workshops, which can bring you into contact with people and ideas that have the power to shape your professional future. You will have the opportunity to learn about the work that is going on in different fields of psychology. You will be able to hear professional psychologists and scholars share their experience and knowledge. It is very likely that your involvement in these organizations will help you to decide on your own career goals. It may be possible for you to meet and interact with psychologists who can help you in a variety of ways. You might become so excited by their work that you decide you want to study with them and get involved in their research. You may find a mentor, someone who can help guide you, even during the application process. Such mentors can be helpful to any applicant, but women and members of ethnic minorities have found such individuals to be particularly valuable in finding programs that are good matches. Later, when you are comparing programs, psychological association members may have important information about a program's reputation in a particular area of study.

So, in summary, extracurricular activities may be less important as a credential to list on your application than as an avenue for acquiring information and contacts that will enable you to enhance your attractiveness as an applicant, to choose the programs that are the best fit your interests, and ultimately to succeed in your graduate school endeavors.

Unspecified Criteria

"Unspecified criteria" refers to those criteria that are not directly stated by programs but that can indirectly influence your status as an applicant, either positively or negatively. One such criterion is a resume. Although inclusion of a resume with your application form is usually optional, we recommend it for three reasons: (a) A resume concisely summarizes the most pertinent information about you in an easy-to-read format, (b) most people who write letters of recommendation prefer to have them to refer to, and (c) most programs will appreciate the fact that you were willing to take this extra step (see chapter 6).

Another unspecified criterion is the quality of your application materials, which includes neatness, readability, completeness, timeliness, accuracy, and so forth. Plan to type rather than write on the application form, and be sure to allow enough time to proofread any materials you submit. Anything other than a perfectly rendered application may be seen as a lack of professionalism (again, see chapter 6).

School and work-site behaviors and attitudes are important factors that can influence the number of options you have regarding letters of recommendation. Good experiences with teachers and supervisors increase the chances of putting together an impressive set of letters, whereas negative experiences will limit your options in that regard.

Successful completion of special projects or honors courses may be considered an asset because they are an indication of higher abilities and initiative. Programs may consider such activities if you are otherwise evenly matched with your competitors on objective and nonobjective criteria.

Finally, most programs value diversity and are aware that some groups are underrepresented in psychology, therefore limiting research about these populations and mental health services to them. There is also a great need for ethnic minority members in academia and in research, both to train the next generation of psychologists and to ensure that the research base is relevant to ethnic minority concerns. Although a minority status will never in itself secure a place for you in graduate school, you should be aware that many programs are committed to recruiting highly qualified students who are also members of minority groups (see chapter 5).

Conclusion

In this chapter, we have looked at the primary criteria by which applicants are evaluated. We have seen how GPAs, standardized test scores, and coursework are evaluated in the context of such other factors as letters of recommendation, research and field-related work experience, application essays, and extracurricular activities. We have also briefly touched on some factors that indirectly affect admission decisions, such as a meticulous attention to the preparation of application materials.

For most readers, this is a sobering process. You may become aware of regrets about the past. You may wish you had partied less and studied harder and smarter early in undergraduate school, for example, so that you could boast a better GPA. You might regret that unpaid research opportunity you passed up to work more hours on your retail sales job. You can take some solace in the fact that in that regard you're definitely not alone. Hindsight is always 20/20. What is more important than the past, however, is a realistic assessment of your current status according to these criteria and a practical plan for redressing your weaknesses and strategically choosing programs that will most likely appreciate your assets.

In this chapter, we have looked at some ways of bolstering your credentials. In the next chapter, we again turn the lens around by helping you decide which criteria *you* will use to judge programs. Then we walk you through the process of researching programs in order to rate them according to both sets of criteria: what you are looking for in a program and what a program is looking for in you. As a result, you will be able to identify those few programs that most precisely fit who you are and who you hope to be.

Choosing Which Programs To Apply To

One cannot collect all the beautiful shells on the beach; one can collect only a few, and they are more beautiful if they are few.
—*Anne Morrow Lindbergh*

Choosing the right programs to apply to is at the heart of every successful application strategy. Not only will this decision strongly influence your chances of gaining admission to graduate school, it will also affect your probability of success in attaining your degree and achieving your career objectives. Thus, program selection should be a rational process that leads you to choose the best possible matches between you and the programs available.

When you have finished this chapter, you will have systematically chosen from hundreds of graduate psychology programs, less than one dozen to which you will actually apply. How do you begin? You begin with a plan. And this chapter provides a ready-made one in the form of seven manageable steps. Each step will be presented in detail in the discussion that follows, but we will first present a brief overview of the process.

Overview

In general, you will follow the same iterative approach you have followed in previous chapters—looking at yourself, then at programs, then again at yourself, and so on. First, you will complete an applicant worksheet that summarizes what you are looking for in a program and what you have to offer in terms of qualifications. Second, you will select from *Grad Study* those programs that are congruent with your requirements and qualifications. Third, you will use *Grad Study* to complete program worksheets that will contain essential data for each program. Fourth, on the basis of these data, you will narrow down your list of programs to those that are strong bets, good bets, and long shots. Fifth, you will contact these programs to obtain additional information and application materials. Sixth, on the basis of this information, you will make a final choice of programs to which you will apply. Finally, you will decide whether a campus visit will be needed to confirm your program selections.

Although this may at first glance seem to be a lot of work, if you have been actively evaluating yourself and your career and training needs in chapters 2 through 4, you have done much of the work already. In the early steps in this chapter, you will simply formalize and make accessible on paper what you have previously learned. In the latter steps, you need only apply this knowledge in a systematic way to the selection of programs. If you are able to find someone who will help you track your progress on each step, the process will be easier still.

As you work through each of these steps, budget your time carefully, so that you don't overspend your resources on the earlier steps or short-change yourself on the latter ones, particularly if you are reading this chapter in September of your senior year or later. And, because this is hard work, reward yourself in small ways for each step that you take. You might promise yourself a movie after you've completed step 5.1, for example. You might go out to dinner with a friend or family member after step 5.4. Each completion will infuse you with more energy to go on to the next step. So let's begin.

Step 5.1: Organize Your Training Requirements, Qualifications, and Program Preferences

Sometimes, when you're immersed in anxiety about high admission standards and competition, you can forget that you owe it to yourself to be as selective as the schools are. After all, it's your whole future that is at stake, and you deserve the best match you can make. During this selection process, you will be gathering a large amount of complex information, so you will need some way to organize your findings. We suggest that you begin by using an applicant worksheet on which you can summarize your qualifications and the factors that will influence your program selections. Such a worksheet will help you organize your thoughts, and it will be a valuable tool later for choosing programs, filling out your applications, and preparing for interviews.

The sample applicant worksheet in Exhibit 5.1 is a prototype. It provides suggested headings for the categories of information that you might want to include in your own summary worksheet. We have arranged the worksheet into three sections to approximate the relative importance that the information should have in your decision making. That is, as you progress from making preliminary selections to final selections, you should first consider your training requirements, then your qualifications, and, finally, your program preferences on other dimensions, such as faculty interests and geographical location.

Feel free to photocopy the worksheet (you may want to use a photocopier with an enlarging capability for this and other forms in this book) or to customize it to suit your own needs. For example, under qualifications, students who already have a PhD and who want to respecialize would need to modify the coursework section to focus on graduate courses rather than undergraduate ones. International students might add a category under training requirements related to the TOEFL (see Resources).

Training Requirements

In this area of your worksheet, you should first designate a program area and a degree (e.g., an MA in human factors engineering or a PhD in clinical psychology). Next, you should decide which of the three training models you prefer. This is a relatively less important decision than is choosing a program area and a degree, but the two are in some ways interrelated. If you want to do substantial research in child development as well as practice child psychology, for example, your best choice might be a clinical psychology program that follows the scientist–practitioner training model and offers a PhD. If you find yourself stuck in identifying programs, degrees, and training models that are right for you, you may want to reread chapter 3 and to talk with other people in the field, perhaps by making an appointment with a psychology professor at a local university. It will be very difficult, if not impossible, to begin weeding out clearly inappropriate programs unless you have made firm decisions about which program area you want to concentrate on and which degree you want to earn.

At this time, you should also begin to give some thought to the kind of reputation you wish a program to have. One study of clinical psychology doctoral students, for example, found that the reputation of the program was the most important reason students gave for making a final choice of programs (Walfish, Stenmark, Shealy, & Shealy, 1989). These researchers also noted, however, that identifying programs with the best reputation is a subjective process that can be quite difficult. Your task at this point is only to begin to identify the *kind* of reputation that is im-

Exhibit 5.1

Applicant Worksheet

1. TRAINING REQUIREMENTS

Degree Desired _____

Area of Concentration _____

Training Model Preferred (check as many as applicable)

_____ Research Scientist _____ Scientist–Practitioner _____ Professional

Program Reputation (List important aspects) _____

_____

Other _____

_____

2. QUALIFICATIONS
Objective Criteria

Coursework:

Psychology Courses (List individually with number of credits in
parentheses): _____

_____

_____

_____

Other Science Courses _____

_____

Mathematics and Statistics Courses _____

_____

Computer Science Courses _____

Honors Courses _____

Other Courses _____

Grades:

Overall GPA _____

Psychology GPA _____

Last 2 Years' GPA _____

Standardized Test Scores:

Gre-Verbal (V) _____

GRE-Quantitative (Q) _____

GRE-Analytical _____

GRE-V + Q _____

GRE-Psychology _____

MAT _____

continued

Exhibit 5.1, continued

Nonobjective Criteria

Candidates for letters of recommendation

_____

_____

_____

_____

_____

_____

_____

Experience (paid or volunteer)

Research _____

Field-Related _____

Clinical and Human Services _____

Extracurricular Activities _____

_____

Personal Characteristics _____

_____

_____

Summary of Strengths and Weaknesses

Strengths _____

_____

Weaknesses _____

_____

3. PROGRAM PREFERENCES

Faculty Interests _____

Special Populations _____

Accreditation _____

Geographical Location _____

Disability-Related Needs _____

Financial Considerations

Sources of Financial Support _____

Types of Financial Aid to Consider _____

Mentors _____

Other Factors to Consider _____

_____

Table 5.1

Measures of Quality in Graduate Education

Faculty

Academic training
Research activity
Research productivity
Teaching effectiveness
Concern for student development and welfare
Involvement in program affairs
Group morale or esprit

Students

Academic ability at entrance
Achievements, knowledge, skills at time of degree completion
Professional accomplishments of graduates
Judgments on program quality
Satisfactions with various aspects of program
Group morale or esprit

Resources

Financial support—internal and external
Library
Laboratory equipment and facilities
Computer facilities

Operations

Purposes of the program
Course and program offerings
Admissions policies
Faculty welfare
Evaluation of student progress
Program leadership and decision making
Job placement of graduates
Advisement of students
Student–faculty interaction
Internships, assistantships, and other opportunities for relevant student experiences
Degree requirements
Relationships with cognate programs
Efficiency of degree production

Note. Items in this table were judged by deans of graduate schools to be "closely related to educational quality" of graduate programs and to be "amenable to measurement." They are from a study conducted for the Council of Graduate Schools by three research psychologists at the Educational Testing Service (Clark, M. J., Hartnett, R. T., & Baird, L. L., *Assessing Dimensions of Quality in Doctoral Education.* Princeton, NJ: Educational Testing Service, 1976, p. 1.8. Copyright 1976 by the Educational Testing Service. Reprinted by permission).

portant to you. Table 5.1 presents four categories of qualities on which a graduate program's reputation might be based: faculty, students, resources, and operations (Clark, Hartnett, & Baird, 1976). Although the study is somewhat dated now, most of the categories and items are still relevant. Read this table carefully and record under reputation the ones that seem essential to you. (Criteria that seem important but not essential will be listed under program preferences.)

Finally, the "Other" category under Training Requirements can be

Table 5.2

Weighted Rankings Based on Number of Times Ranked Among the Top Five Reasons for Making a Final Decision

Item	Ranking					Total points
	1	2	3	4	5	
Amount of clinical supervision	23	15	13	13	14	254
Amount of research supervision	4	10	5	6	11	98
Amount of stipend offered	15	17	18	19	13	248
Appropriate mentors available	5	9	15	14	7	141
Break required during program	3	2	1	1	1	29
Diversity of program	12	13	13	10	2	173
Emotional atmosphere of the program	10	11	17	22	17	206
Expected length of program	2	2	9	6	9	66
Family/significant others in area	16	8	7	7	9	156
Geographic location	15	9	9	11	7	167
Number of minority members in program	0	1	2	0	3	13
Recreational activities available	0	0	2	2	4	14
Reputation of the program	22	24	14	23	24	318
Research experiences available	6	11	12	15	8	148
Specific professor to work with	17	11	5	1	8	154
Specific specialty training available	18	7	10	4	4	160
Specificity of the training program	1	9	1	7	2	60
Success of previous graduates	0	2	7	9	9	56
Theoretical orientation	14	7	10	12	16	168
Training facilities available	8	11	15	10	14	163
Tuition waiver available	8	19	13	6	13	180

Note. Reprinted with permission from "Reasons Why Applicants Select Clinical Psychology Programs," by S. Walfish, D. E. Stenmark, J. S. Shealy, and S. E. Shealy, 1989, *Professional Psychology: Research and Practice, 20,* p. 352.

used to highlight additional aspects of a training program that are important to some students. Table 5.2, from Walfish et al. (1989), lists additional criteria that clinical psychology students used to choose among programs. It's important to note that the highest ranked criteria after the reputation of a program for clinical students were the amount of clinical supervision and the emotional atmosphere of a program. (Research psychology students might be more interested in the amount and kinds of research opportunities a program offers.) Look through this table, identify only the criteria that are essential to you, and list these under "Other." (Again, criteria that seem important but not essential will be listed under program preferences.)

Qualifications

Under "Objective Criteria," you will want to record first your coursework: the number and type of psychology courses; other science courses; and mathematics, statistics, and computer science courses you have taken. Next, list any honors courses you may have attended. List under "Other" courses that do not fall into any of these areas but may be relevant to psychology. In parentheses in each category, note those classes you plan to attend by the time that you apply. Then, using your undergraduate transcript, calculate your overall GPA, the GPA you received in psychology courses only, and the GPA for the last two years of your undergraduate program. Depending on whether you have graduated, this calculation will be more or less complete.

Finally, list standardized test scores if you have already taken the GREs and the MAT, or make a working estimate based on your performance on diagnostic and practice tests. (If you have not yet obtained one of the guides for these exams and taken a diagnostic test, now would be a good time to do so.)

Under "Nonobjective Criteria," brainstorm options for letters of recommendation (you will select from this list in the next chapter). Under each person's name, jot down which of your qualifications that person is in a position to address. You should list a minimum of three people, and more if possible. If you are unsure whom to ask, reread the relevant section of chapter 4.

Also note the experiences you have had or plan to have by the time you apply, paid or volunteer. Any extracurricular activities related to psychology that you have been involved in should be listed next, followed by any special class projects you have been involved in, such as a senior thesis. Again, rereading chapter 4 can be helpful when you're not sure whether to include an experience on your worksheet.

When you think through personal characteristics, be honest but don't be self-effacing. You will need to sell yourself in your application essay and in your interviews. Think over your school, work, and social experiences. What talents, skills, and abilities have you exhibited? In what ways did you shine? For which personal characteristics have you gotten positive feedback in the past from teachers or supervisors on a job? Are you mature, independent, or highly motivated? Are you a curious person? Are you known for being organized? Do you often show initiative or take a leadership position? By listing these personal attributes, you lay the groundwork for presenting yourself effectively in essays and in interviews later on.

Finally, when you have listed all of this information, you may want to summarize your strengths and weaknesses (e.g., strong GPA but no research experience; strong letters of recommendation but relatively low GREs) at the bottom of this section of the form. This summary will be helpful when you are narrowing down the programs to which you will apply.

Program Preferences

In this final section of the worksheet, you will list those characteristics of programs that are not essential but that are important to you and thus may very well influence your final choices. In addition to the categories we have delineated in this section, you should also add any areas you identified as important but not essential as you were completing the first part of this worksheet. If the categories we have delineated are not applicable to you, just indicate n/a on the form.

Faculty Interests

Under "Faculty Interests" you should list specific areas of interest to you that you might want faculty to share. For example, a clinical student might have a special interest in the treatment of a particular disorder (e.g., posttraumatic stress disorder) or a particular population (e.g., children); a human factors student might eventually want to focus on highway safety. Record here only those interests that have been compelling to you for some time, not attractions that are likely to pass. Although it is not essential that a program have faculty who represent these areas, shared interests can be important when looking for a mentor (see later discussion) or when lining up a chairman and committee for your dissertation or thesis (Cone & Foster, 1993). At the same time, be aware that faculty often leave one university to take another position and also that your interests are likely to change to some degree once you are in an actual program. Overall, however, programs look for students whose interests "fit" with those of the current program faculty.

Specific Populations

In a related vein, you might also begin to think through whether you are particularly interested in research about or service to some specific population, such as women; members of ethnic minority groups; gay, lesbian, and bisexual individuals; or persons with disabilities. Although we touched on this in earlier chapters, it merits additional attention here because for many students, it may be a key consideration in selecting programs. If you are a member of any of these specific groups or if you are simply interested in working with a particular population, you should decide at this point how important it is to you to (a) be in an environment with others like yourself and (b) be working with faculty who do research about or provide services to these populations. These are decisions that involve values as well as interests and that sometimes even involve politics. As we proceed with these steps, you will see how these decisions come into play at several points. For now, you don't need to make a final commitment, you just need to have some idea of whether this will be a relevant point for you to consider in evaluating programs.

Accreditation

The APA accredits only clinical, counseling, and school psychology programs. So if you select a program other than these, APA accreditation will be irrelevant to you. Even if you are interested in these types of programs, accreditation status may be more important to some students than to others. Those who want to become licensed clinicians may be interested only in programs that are accredited if this is required for licensure in the states they may want to practice. Those who want to teach at the university level in these areas might feel more secure if they achieve a doctoral degree from an accredited program. You should note, however, that accredited programs frequently have higher admissions standards than those that are not accredited.

Geographical Location

Geographical location may be important to people in different ways. For many, family status has a strong bearing on geographical preferences. If you are in a committed relationship, for example, you may only want to apply in geographical areas where your partner is likely to find a job in his or her field. If you have children, you might also want to look at the reputation of the day-care centers and public school systems in various states in which you are considering psychology programs. If you are a single parent with a strong support system where you are, you may want to stay within a certain geographic radius of these supports. Individual status might also influence geographical preferences. Women and others with custody of children may not want to attend a university in a city with a high crime rate. Gay and lesbian individuals who value being part of a relatively large gay community may want to choose geographical areas accordingly. And some minority students prefer to stay close to their cultural roots and extended families (e.g., some Native Americans). Geography can intersect with training issues as well. If you are a human factors student wanting to do research on defense aerospace systems, for example, you may want your program located near (and perhaps affiliated with) a large military base.

Disability-Related Needs

We include disability-related needs under program preferences rather than training requirements, because they should be considered *after* students have selected programs according to their training needs and interests. Graduate programs are required by law to provide the same kinds of accessibility as are undergraduate programs and other forms of higher education. Those who have been disabled for some time are probably quite conversant with the law, but those who are more recently disabled might benefit from familiarizing themselves with the Rehabilitation Act of 1973 (PL 93–112, particularly Section 504) and the Americans With Disabilities Act of 1990. Basically, among other things, both of these laws state that all entities receiving federal funds (which includes nearly all colleges and universities) must provide accommodations to make programs accessible to otherwise qualified persons with disabilities. For graduate students with disabilities, adjustment required by the law may include changes in the way specific courses are conducted and the ways tests are administered and may involve the use of specialized equipment and support staff.

For further information related to these laws and to higher education and students with disabilities, the HEATH (Higher Education and Adult Training for People With Handicaps) Resource Center is an excellent source of information. They publish a newsletter twice a year, and have an extensive publication program, a toll-free telephone service, and a professional staff with a network of colleagues across the country (see Resources).

Students who were disabled when they sought admission as undergraduates should ask the same kinds of questions they asked (or wished they had asked) then. More recently disabled students should use their broader experience as a guide, should read education-related publications such as *How to Choose a College: A Guide for the Student With a Disability* (see Resources), and should talk to other disabled students, if possible, to come up with a list of questions. A student who uses a wheelchair, for example, might ask if there is an adapted transportation system on campus. A student with a hearing impairment might ask who makes arrangements for interpreters and whether interpreters are available for nonclassroom activities such as practica. A student with a visual impairment might ask what kind of arrangements there are to take tests with a reader (Jarrow et al., 1991).

A common tendency of disabled graduate students is to feel that they should ask for or get along with less assistance at this higher level of education. This can be unrealistic and unproductive. Be down-to-earth when you list disability-related needs. *All* students need *all* the resources they can muster to succeed in a rigorous graduate program such as psychology.

Financial Considerations

Moving to the next item on the applicant worksheet, financial considerations, you should at this point list the amount and sources of financial support that you will already have (e.g., savings, partner's income, family support). You should also begin thinking about the estimated cost of each year of graduate study (refer to chapter 2 for ballpark figures; in step 5.3, you will get more specific information on particular programs).

You might also begin to familiarize yourself with the kinds of aid available. Most graduate student financial aid falls into one of four categories: tuition waivers; scholarships, grants, and fellowships; research and teaching assistantships and traineeships; and loans. Tuition waivers (full and partial), common in many educational institutions, do just that—they absolve the student from paying tuition and sometimes fees, and they are usually granted on a yearly basis through the university, graduate school, psychology department, or particular psychology program, often in conjunction with other financial aid (e.g., assistantships), and with or without a requirement of service repayment. Scholarships, grants, and fellowships can be either need or merit based and can be from the university, department, or program or from another institutional source. Funds received through these awards typically do not require concurrent work activities on the student's part. Research and teaching assistantships and traineeships do require such work, however, and they are usually administered through the psychology department or specific program within the department. The number of hours you will work varies depending on the type of assistantship and the financial compensation and on the psychologist who oversees the actual work. Research assistantships may require that you help run experiments and record and analyze data, and some require that you supervise undergraduate research. Teaching assistantships typically involve administering and grading exams and papers and may require you to actually lecture in an undergraduate course in psychology, to lead discussion groups, or to serve as a laboratory instructor. Traineeships are often work positions in a public or private organization, either within or outside of the university, that involve basic and applied research and psychology-related services. Many of these assistantships and traineeships are directly related to your educational goals, so rather than being a burden, such work can be a boon. Loans are the fourth major source of aid in graduate school. These are funds borrowed from banks, state educational loan authorities, or the federal government, which typically have a low interest rate and can be paid off over an extended period of time. In addition to knowing about these general types of aid, students from specific populations, such as members of ethnic minorities, should also be aware that some awards have been specifically earmarked for them in order to encourage their participation in the field (see also step 5.5). On the other hand, students with disabilities are often disappointed to find that much of the disability-related financial support, such as vocational rehabilitation funds, they may have received as undergraduates is not available to them as graduate students.

Table 5.3 shows the various sources of financial support for doctoral training reported by 1991 doctorate recipients in psychology. As is indicated, the majority of graduate students incur some amount of debt during graduate school, even when they receive other sources of aid. Table 5.4 shows the level of education-related debt owed at the time of receipt of the doctoral degree by 1991 psychology doctorate recipients who reported any debt. For now, simply peruse these data and become familiar with the idea that as you apply to programs, you will also be attempting to put together a package of aid for the several years you will be in graduate school. As we will stress again later in this chapter, there are many creative ways to finance your education. Some of the more expensive schools also have the most extensive financial aid opportunities, so no student should rule out any particular program at this point because of financial concerns.

Mentors
Mentoring is listed here so that you will give some thought to its potential value to you. Briefly, mentors serve as guides and have interpersonal, organizational, and systems functions, according to Gilbert and Rossman (1992). Activities in the interpersonal sphere include role modeling; ac-

Table 5.3

Sources of Financial Support for Doctoral Training Reported by 1991 Doctorate Recipients in Psychology

Source of Support	All Sources[a]		Primary Source	
	N	%	N	%
Own family resources				
Own earnings	1834	85.2	370	17.2
Spouse's earnings	908	42.2	251	11.7
Family contributions	844	39.2	128	5.9
Other personal sources	175	8.1	35	1.6
Subtotal[b]	2024	94.0	784	36.4
Student loans				
Guaranteed Student Loan	1142	53.0	217	10.1
H.E.A.L.	102	4.7	10	.5
National Direct Student Loan	339	15.7	6	.3
Other loan	178	8.3	6	.3
Subtotal[b]	1225	56.9	239	11.1
University-related sources				
Teaching assistantship	1107	51.4	199	9.2
Research assistantship	850	39.5	143	6.6
Fellowship	495	23.0	60	2.8
Other university source	238	11.1	41	1.9
Subtotal[b]	1542	71.6	443	20.6
Federal sources				
NIMH traineeship	163	7.6	24	1.1
NIH traineeship	28	1.3	8	.4
NSF fellowship	22	1.0	12	.6
NSF research assistantship	14	.7	3	.1
NIH research assistantship	26	1.2	1	.0
Other HHS sources	9	.4	2	.1
G*POP	14	.7	5	.2
Other Department of Education	9	.4	1	.0
VA (GI Bill etc.)	32	1.5	2	.1
Other U.S. federal	48	2.2	4	.2
Canadian Provincial/Federal Fellow	50	2.3	26	1.2
Other federal	10	.5	5	.2
Subtotal[b]	375	17.4	93	4.3

continued

Table 5.3, continued

Source of Support	All Sources[a]		Primary Source	
	N	%	N	%
Other sources	160	7.4	27	1.3
No sources specified	23	1.1	567	26.4
Total	2153	100.0	2153	100.0

Note. H.E.A.L. = Health Education Assistance Loan; NIMH = National Institute of Mental Health; NIH = National Institutes of Health; NSF = National Science Foundation; HHS = Department of Health and Human Services; G*POP = Graduate Professional Opportunities Program Fellowships; VA = Veterans Administration. Source: *1991 Doctorate Employment Survey*, Office of Demographic, Employment, and Educational Research, APA Education Directorate.
[a] Respondents were given the opportunity to indicate all sources of financial support, and many indicated more than one source. Therefore, the percentages in this column total more than 100.0%. [b] These entries indicate the number and percentage of respondents who indicated any personal, student loan, university-related, or federal source of support.

ceptance, confirmation, and empowerment; counseling; and friendship. At the organizational and systems level, mentoring may include sponsoring, coaching, and protecting the student and introducing the student to important others. For example, the mentor can model adherence to standards of performance and codes of ethics and can also help the student gain visibility and status within a particular network, helping to increase professional opportunities and the student's self-confidence (Cronan-Hillix, Gensheimer, Cronan-Hillix, & Davidson, 1986).

Some have heralded mentorship as the "key to a rewarding graduate career" (Cesa & Fraser, 1989). There is also some evidence that mentorship increases a student's predoctoral productivity (Crane, 1965; Reskin, 1979; both cited in Cronan-Hillix et al., 1986) and influences initial job placement (Long, 1978; cited in Cesa & Fraser, 1989). Informally, many students have described mentors as helping them to stay with their graduate programs when the going got tough and to successfully complete their theses and dissertations in a reasonable amount of time.

How does one increase one's chances of finding such a mentor? One study (Cronan-Hillix et al., 1986) indicated that 80% of students who sought out mentors did so on the basis of similar interests. So, if a mentoring relationship appeals to you, when researching programs you may want to pay particular attention to the number of faculty that appear to have interests similar to your own. If you are a woman, you might con-

Table 5.4

Level of Education-Related Debt Owed Upon Receipt of Doctoral Degree: 1991 Doctorate Recipients in Psychology Who Reported Any Debt

Area of study in psychology	Level of cumulative debt at graduation																		Total N
	$5K or less		$6–10 K		$11–15K		$16–20K		$21–30K		$31–40K		$41–50K		$51–75K		More than $75,000		
	N	%	N	%	N	%	N	%	N	%	N	%	N	%	N	%	N	%	
Clinical	89	12.8	95	13.6	91	13.1	72	10.3	147	21.1	81	11.6	62	8.9	42	6.0	18	2.6	697
Clinical Neuropsychology	4	17.4	4	17.4	1	4.3	0	0.0	6	26.1	2	8.7	2	8.7	3	13.0	1	4.3	23
Community	1	14.3	4	57.1	0	0.0	1	14.3	0	0.0	1	14.3	0	0.0	0	0.0	0	0.0	7
Counseling	32	19.3	35	21.1	30	18.1	26	15.7	23	13.9	15	9.0	1	0.6	3	1.8	1	0.6	166
Health	1	7.1	6	42.9	0	0.0	5	35.7	0	0.0	2	14.3	0	0.0	0	0.0	0	0.0	14
School	15	21.7	18	26.1	13	18.8	9	13.0	9	13.0	4	5.8	1	1.4	0	0.0	0	0.0	69
Biological/Physiological/ Comparative/Psycho- pharmacology	6	31.6	4	21.1	5	26.3	3	15.8	1	5.3	0	0.0	0	0.0	0	0.0	0	0.0	19
Cognitive	12	27.3	14	31.8	6	13.6	6	13.6	5	11.4	0	0.0	0	0.0	0	0.0	1	2.3	44
Developmental	10	16.9	21	35.6	10	16.9	7	11.9	10	16.9	1	1.7	0	0.0	0	0.0	0	0.0	59
Educational	7	18.9	9	24.3	7	18.9	6	16.2	5	13.5	2	5.4	1	2.7	0	0.0	0	0.0	37
Experimental	14	37.8	8	21.6	5	13.5	3	8.1	4	10.8	2	5.4	1	2.7	0	0.0	0	0.0	37
General	2	15.4	3	23.1	2	15.4	3	23.1	1	7.7	1	7.7	0	0.0	1	7.7	0	0.0	13
Industrial/Organizational	11	18.6	13	22.0	14	23.7	5	8.5	10	16.9	4	6.8	1	1.7	1	1.7	0	0.0	59
Neurosciences	3	27.3	4	36.4	1	9.1	1	9.1	1	9.1	0	0.0	1	9.1	0	0.0	0	0.0	11
Personality	2	28.6	2	28.6	2	28.6	0	0.0	0	0.0	1	14.3	0	0.0	0	0.0	0	0.0	7
Psychometrics	2	50.0	0	0.0	0	0.0	0	0.0	2	50.0	0	0.0	0	0.0	0	0.0	0	0.0	4
Quantitative	2	33.3	0	0.0	3	50.0	0	0.0	1	16.7	0	0.0	0	0.0	0	0.0	0	0.0	6
Social	15	23.8	17	27.0	10	15.9	9	14.3	8	12.7	2	3.2	1	1.6	1	1.6	0	0.0	63
Other in psychology	16	29.1	16	29.1	3	5.5	7	12.7	6	10.9	2	3.6	3	5.5	1	1.8	1	1.8	55
Other not psychology	2	12.5	6	37.5	3	18.8	3	18.8	1	6.3	1	6.3	0	0.0	0	0.0	0	0.0	16
Not specified	8	20.0	7	17.5	7	17.5	7	17.5	3	7.5	5	12.5	3	7.5	0	0.0	0	0.0	40
Total	254	17.6	286	19.8	213	14.7	173	12.0	243	16.8	126	8.7	77	5.3	52	3.6	22	1.5	1,446

Source: *1991 Doctorate Employment Survey*, Office of Demographic, Employment, and Educational Research, APA Education Directorate.

sider, in addition, the benefits of same-sex mentoring. For example, a female mentor may not only help a student succeed in graduate school, but may also model how to integrate career achievement with successful family life (Gilbert & Rossman, 1992). Similarly, members of underrepresented groups in psychology, such as ethnic minorities, can help students integrate their ethnic identity with various professional roles. So, if you are a woman or a member of a minority population who wishes to have a same-sex or same-ethnicity mentor, you may want to pay particular attention to the percentage of full-time female and ethnic minority faculty in a particular program.[1] An alternative to searching for a same-sex or same-group mentor may be to learn from other students the faculty who have good track records with working with different populations of students. The more of such individuals in a particular program, the greater the chance that you will find a satisfying mentoring relationship.

Other Factors to Consider

As your last task in this step, consider other factors that may be important to you. These should include areas that seemed important but not essential when you were completing the first section of the worksheet, as well as others that occur to you now. You may want to make sure that a clinical program also has a focus on prevention, for example. You may be enamored of a particular theoretical orientation and would like a program that stresses that. You may decide that you would like a certain percentage of graduate students to be members of minority groups, not just for the support that may provide, but also for the opportunity to work with other students performing research about or providing services to a particular ethnic population. If you are a gay, lesbian, or bisexual student, you will need to decide whether you need a program where it feels safe to be out. If you are a student with a disability, you may be particularly concerned with the transportation system in any geographical area in which you might study. Older students who are returning to school at midlife may have a strong need to "get in and get out" of a program quickly. For these students, the track record of a program with regard to how many years it typically takes a student to graduate might be quite important to know.

In considering these other preferences, also let your past experience

---

1. Although we could find no hard evidence that same-sex or same-ethnicity mentorship confers greater benefits to students, this may be because mentoring has only recently become a subject of research.

be your guide.[2] What allowed you to succeed in undergraduate school or in a difficult job? Did a particular individual or group help you through? What kind of support or environment did you wish you had that you didn't have then? Did being at a large school overwhelm you or did being at a small school hem you in? What would your "ideal" situation be?

Although we will discuss the mechanics of researching programs on these dimensions of program preferences later in this chapter, for now it is enough that you begin to identify such aspects as being important in your search. Identifying them now will make the job of selecting programs to which to apply much easier later on.

Step 5.2: Compile a Preliminary List of Programs That Offer the Area of Concentration, Degree, and Training That You Seek

Graduate Study in Psychology is the main resource specifically designed to assist students in identifying and choosing graduate programs in psychology. We strongly recommend this publication as your primary resource in this step. A secondary resource that you may find helpful for library use is *Peterson's Annual Guides to Graduate Study* (see Resources). International students should also consult *The College Handbook Foreign Students' Supplement* and *The Guide to State Residency Requirements* (see Resources). These publications can be purchased by mail and are readily found in the reference sections of university and public libraries and college career counseling centers (see Resources). Several divisions of the APA have information on training in certain areas of concentration. You may call Division Services (see Resources) to find out if there is training-related material in your area of interest.

The APA also publishes several resources for specific populations. The Association's Women's Program publishes *Graduate Faculty Interested in the Psychology of Women*. It includes information on faculty involved in research on the psychology of women, women of color, and the clinical assessment/treatment concerns of women. It also includes information on curricula and faculty appointments in the psychology of women; women's study programs; and the sex and ethnicity of full-time faculty. These data are provided for both master's and doctoral programs in psychology. The APA's Committee on Lesbian and Gay Concerns publishes a similar vol-

---

2. We thank Robin Soler for the following list of questions.

ume, *Graduate Faculty in Psychology Interested in Lesbian and Gay Issues*. It lists doctoral and master's programs with research related to lesbian and gay issues; master's and doctoral programs with courses placing significant emphasis on lesbian and gay issues; master's and doctoral programs with training and supervision for providing services to lesbian and gay clients; and student organizations on campus and openly self-identified students and faculty according to state, institution, and program. These kinds of guides can be particularly useful in starting your search if being part of or working with a specific population is a priority for you.

An expedient way to begin to compile a preliminary list of programs is to scan the "Index of Programs by Area of Study Offered" in the back of *Grad Study* and make a mark next to those programs that offer the particular area of concentration and degree you are seeking. The size of your preliminary list will depend on how common your interest area is. For example, environmental psychology may yield only a dozen possibilities, whereas clinical psychology may yield more than 300. Students who already have a PhD in psychology and are seeking to respecialize in clinical psychology will find "Clinical Respecialization" in the index. Those wishing to reconcentrate in another area, such as forensic psychology, neuropsychology, school psychology, health psychology, and so on, will need to locate programs offering that kind of training generally and then contact the programs to see whether they offer the opportunity to respecialize.

Step 5.3: Research Programs on Your List

Devising a Program Worksheet

To analyze your preliminary possibilities, we suggest that you use a program worksheet similar to the applicant worksheet you used in step 5.1. You will maintain separate worksheets for each program (not school or department, because more than one program may be housed in the same institution) that you are intending to investigate. This strategy has several advantages:

- Having a worksheet will save you the time of writing down the same headings repeatedly for numerous programs.
- A worksheet can also be used as a checklist to ensure that you have acquired all of the pertinent information for each program.

Exhibit 5.2

Program Worksheet

BASIC DATA

Name of University and Department _____

Name of Program _____

Accreditation Status _____

Year Department Established _____ Number of Full-Time Faculty _____

Degree(s) Offered in Relevant Program _____

Phone Number and Address to Send Application _____

_____

Application Deadline and Fee _____

Number of Applications to Program _____ Number Accepted _____

Percentage of Students in Relevant Minority Group _____

Retention Rate (General) _____ (Special Populations) _____

Degree Requirements _____

ADMISSION REQUIREMENTS

Coursework
(R = required; P = preferred)

Your Qualifications

Below   Meet   Exceed

Psychology (Note whether R or P)

_____

_____

_____

_____

_____

_____

_____

Other Science (Note whether R or P)

_____

Mathematics

_____

Computer Science

_____

Other

_____

continued

Exhibit 5.2, continued

(R = required; P = preferred)

Your Qualifications

Below   Meet   Exceed

Grades

Overall GPA

(R or P) _____

(Median) _____

Psychology GPA

(R or P) _____

(Median) _____

Last 2 Years' GPA

(R or P) _____

(Median) _____

Standardized Test Scores

GRE-V

(R or P) _____

(Median) _____

GRE-Q

(R or P) _____

(Median) _____

GRE-Analytical

(R or P) _____

(Median) _____

GRE-V+Q

(R or P) _____

(Median) _____

GRE-Psychology

(R or P) _____

(Median) _____

MAT

(R or P) _____

(Median) _____

continued

Exhibit 5.2, continued

Your Qualifications

Below   Meet   Exceed

Other Criteria (List and rate high [H],
medium [M], and low [L])

_____

_____

_____

_____

_____

_____

ADDITIONAL PROGRAM INFORMATION

Tuition for Full-Time Study _____

On-Campus Housing (yes or no) _____

Day Care (yes or no) _____

Financial Assistance (List kind and amount, including average number of hours
worked and other details, when applicable) _____

_____

_____

_____

_____

Number of Full-Time Women Faculty _____

Number of Full-Time Minority Faculty _____

    Additional information in this regard: _____

_____

Minority- or Women-Oriented Courses or Curricula _____

_____

Teaching Opportunities (List whether available [A] or required [R])

_____

Orientation, Objectives, and Emphasis _____

_____

continued

Exhibit 5.2, continued

Training Model _____

Philosophy and Objectives _____

_____

_____

Areas of Emphasis _____

_____

Subspecialties Available _____

_____

Opportunities for Interdisciplinary Study _____

_____

Curriculum Information _____

_____

Theoretical Orientation _____

Internship and Practica Opportunities _____

_____

Other _____

_____

Special Facilities or Resources _____

_____

_____

QUESTIONS AND ISSUES FOR FURTHER EXPLORATION

_____

_____

_____

_____

_____

PROS AND CONS

_____

_____

_____

- Worksheets give you a convenient place to record any updated and additional information you obtain.
- Having separate worksheets in the same format will make it easier for you to make comparisons among individual programs, and between your qualifications and requirements and the admission

requirements of the program. You can lay the worksheets side by side and read the same information across entries.

- Worksheets will enable you to easily sort your programs into meaningful categories using any criteria you choose. For example, you can pull out worksheets for those programs that you need more information about. You can separate programs on the basis of accreditation status, geographical location, or financial aid options. Or, when you are ready to select your final programs, you may want to compile three stacks of worksheets for your first, second, and third choices.

Exhibit 5.2 outlines the categories of information you will want to record on your program worksheet. Note that the headings follow the sequence of information provided for each program in *Grad Study*. Because this makes the entries mostly self-explanatory, we will not go into as much detail as we did when we discussed completing the applicant worksheet. At the end of the worksheet, we have provided space for notes and questions and for summarizing pros and cons of each program. Again, you will want to customize this worksheet so that it fits you, eliminating headings that do not apply, adding headings according to the preferences you identified in step 5.1, and allowing appropriate amounts of space for the level of detail you want. Once you have designed your program worksheet or have decided to use ours, photocopy it so that you have one copy for each of the programs you have identified.

Recording and Interpreting Program Data

Begin by reading the *full* entries in *Grad Study* for each of the programs you marked in the previous step. (If there are a large number, you may want to schedule several sessions for this.) Remember that entries may contain descriptions of more than one program, so be sure you obtain the information that pertains to the specific program you are investigating.

First, fill in the basic data about the program, which will take you down to "Admission Requirements" in the *Grad Study* entry. Then, carefully record objective criteria: coursework, GPAs, and standardized test scores. Objective criteria will be listed as either required (R) or preferred (P). Requirements are usually less negotiable than preferences. In addition, for GPAs and test scores, the median rating of students admitted the previous year will be listed in italics after the required or preferred ratings. The median tells you that approximately half of the students accepted scored above the rating indicated and the other half scored below that rating. The median rating is often the most realistic benchmark when considering the match between program requirements and applicant qualifications. (Do not fill in "Your Qualifications" at this point.)

Next, list tuition, housing and day care, and financial assistance information. You will obtain the information about women and minority faculty under "Special Group Considerations" in the entry. "Teaching Opportunities" will give you some idea of the kind of assistantship work available to those who are awarded that kind of financial aid.

Up to this point, you have not had to interpret what you have read; you've simply recorded the information in a straightforward way. When you reach "Additional Comments. Orientation, Objectives, and Emphasis of Department" in the *Grad Study* entry, you will be required to examine the comments more closely to extract and interpret the information you need about the training model, philosophy and objectives of the program, areas of emphasis, subspecialties available, opportunity for interdisciplinary study, curriculum, and theoretical orientation. The comments may only provide some of this information, and what is provided may be subject to interpretation, which is fine for now. Later, when you request information from the actual program, you will be able to fill in missing information and clarify information that is somewhat ambiguous. When you proceed to "Internships" and "Special Facilities or Resources," you will again revert to basic recording.

Appraising Program Matches

After you have completed this information, your primary concern will be to appraise how well the program appears to satisfy the requirements you identified in step 5.1 (we will get to your qualifications in the next step). This means, for example, discerning whether the program offers a concentration of coursework and practica for your area of concentration, grants the degree required for you to pursue your career, emulates the training model and academic philosophy you prefer, and addresses the most important program preferences you have identified. You will want to rule out any programs that are obviously incompatible with your training requirements and major program preferences at this time. For example, if you have a strong interest in the psychology of gender-related issues, and a particular program has neither faculty interested in that area nor coursework addressing it, depending on the number of programs you have, you might want to consider eliminating it from your list.

Some students are tempted to eliminate programs on the basis of tuition costs. Although you should list this information on your worksheet, we urge you not to rule out any programs strictly because of financial considerations at this time. After you have contacted programs in step 5.5, you will have a better sense of the kinds of financial aid that students in a particular program typically receive, and this may show that a seemingly high-cost private school may be as affordable or even more affordable as a state-supported program, for example.

Again, in completing each worksheet, be aware that an entry will not often tell you everything you want to know, that the training model is not always obvious (see chapter 3, Table 3.2), and that the information for any program may be subject to change since the time it was published. So do not rule out a program that appears to have some potential until you have acquired more information (as we have done in Exhibit 5.2, we suggest that you include space on your worksheet for jotting down questions). Once you have exhausted *Grad Study*, you may choose to peruse other sources of information about programs (such as *Peterson's Annual Guides* and the APA's specific populations materials) and add any pertinent information to your worksheet.

Step 5.4: Compare Your Qualifications With Admission Requirements

Eventually, you will need to consider all of the information on both your applicant and program worksheets to get a complete picture of the nature and quality of each program and to determine which ones are the best matches. For now, to narrow down the possibilities, you need to focus strictly on how well you measure up to admission standards, again using *Grad Study* as your primary resource.

So, as you consider the programs that remain on your preliminary list from step 5.3, look at your record of qualifications from your applicant worksheet. Compare your qualifications with each program's requirements, using grades, standardized test scores, and coursework first, which are the criteria that most programs rely on for their initial screening of applicants. This will help you see at a glance how well you measure up to admission standards for each program.

For each of these admission requirements, indicate whether your qualifications meet, exceed, or are below the required/preferred and median ratings. Then estimate your standing on the nonobjective or "other" criteria. Pay particular attention to those criteria the program rates as "high."

Your next step will be to estimate the match between the program's admission requirements and your qualifications by placing each program into one of the categories that follow. Before presenting these categories, we would like to say that the criteria we are suggesting are approximations, not data-based formulas. Use them as general guidelines, rather than as strict rules, for estimating program matches.

1. *Strong bets*: Your grades, scores, and coursework all exceed the required/preferred or median ratings, whichever are higher. You have strengths on one or more nonobjective criteria that the program values highly.
2. *Good bets*: You have the required coursework and your grades and scores exceed the lower of the two ratings (i.e., required/preferred versus the median) but do not exceed the higher. You have strengths on nonobjective criteria that the program values highly.
3. *Long shots*: Your rating on one of the objective criteria falls slightly short of the required/preferred or median rating (whichever is lower). You have compensatory strengths on nonobjective criteria that the program values highly.
4. *Improbables*: Your rating on two or more of the objective criteria falls slightly short of the required/preferred or median rating (whichever is lower) or your rating on one of the objective criteria falls significantly short of the required/preferred or median rating (whichever is lower).

If a program's requirements are unclear, write any questions you may have under "Questions and Answers for Further Exploration" on the program worksheet. Under "Pros and Cons," on this same worksheet, note any discrepancies between program requirements and your qualifications. Finally, indicate at the top of the worksheet in which category you believe the program belongs. After you eliminate the improbable matches, you should have fewer than 40 programs about which you will gather further information.

If you have more than 40, this may be a good time to exclude those that don't meet some of your important program preferences from your applicant worksheet, such as accreditation status, geographical location, or criteria related to being a member of a specific population. Say, for example, that you prefer to go to school on the east coast and that you are a woman who wants to obtain a PhD in clinical psychology, who has a strong interest in gender-related research, and who wants a same-sex mentor. Using the information you have gathered so far, you can probably eliminate quite a few programs at this time.

If, on the other hand, you do not have many programs on your list to begin with, we want to caution you against ruling out any program too hastily before you have obtained more information. Financial considerations are a good case in point, as we mentioned earlier. Physical access is another example: If you are an excellent candidate for a program that does not currently have special accommodations that you require to attend school, it is altogether possible that the program would not only be legally required but may be especially willing to take special steps for you.

Your eventual goal (see step 5.6) is to identify about 10 programs to which you will apply, with the majority being in the "good bet" category and the rest divided between strong bets and long shots. You may have that number or significantly more at this point. Now, you will obtain additional information in order to finalize your list.

Step 5.5: Contact Programs and Individuals Directly to Obtain Additional Information

The information you have gathered up to this point has enabled you to assemble a sound set of possibilities. The schools remaining on your list offer the area of concentration, degree, and training model you desire, and your academic qualifications are within range of their admission requirements. Some appear to address your program preferences. But you still don't know enough about the programs to determine which of them you should actually apply to. This second information-gathering stage is important for getting to know programs more intimately and for finding the optimum matches. Because of differing information needs, some students will find that this step requires more extensive research than will others. But all students will need to obtain at least some additional information at this point.

For example, we have said that the quality of the program should be one of your foremost concerns. But how do you assess the quality of a program? Resources such as *Grad Study* cannot describe the full range of features and services that give the program its character (e.g., the caliber of its faculty members, the emotional atmosphere of the program, the typical number of years to receipt of degree, or the employment success rate of its graduates. Very few of the measures of quality you chose earlier from Table 5.1 can be explored through general resources such as *Grad Study*. For the most part, this kind of information can be obtained only by making direct contact with a program and with individuals who know about the program.

Request Program Information

Contacting Programs Directly

Before you do anything else, write a brief letter directly to the programs you are still interested in, requesting an application and any other program information that is available (addresses can be found in *Grad Study*). In the event that the school or department houses more than one program, be sure you designate which program you are referring to (you can request materials for more than one program). If you are pressed for time, you may be willing to incur the expense of long-distance calls in order to save a few days. In this initial request, do not burden programs with specific or detailed questions. Many of your questions will be answered in the materials they send, and you may write follow-up letters or call with these questions after you have reviewed the information you receive. Be sure, however, to specifically ask about financial aid information administered through the psychology department or program. If there are statistics on how many students received how much aid of what type in recent years, this would be most valuable. It is important to ask for this information now because the deadlines for applying for financial aid may be *earlier* than application deadlines.

When you make your first and subsequent contacts with a program, remember that you will be giving that program the opportunity to form impressions of you; therefore, how you conduct yourself is extremely important. Prepare your letters requesting information with care, using formal business letter form, typing neatly, and so forth. Remember, it is important to make a good first impression. It could be a lasting impression: These letters are often kept in the same file as your application, once it is received.

There is no standard response time for receiving information or applications. Expect to wait an average of 2–4 weeks for a reply. It would not be impolite to call a program if you do not receive materials within 4 weeks. Some programs may ask for a fee before sending materials, and a few may actually want more information about you before sending you an application.

Respecialization Applicants

If you have a doctoral degree in psychology and are hoping to respecialize, you should read "Policy on Training for Psychologists Wishing to Change Their Specialty," printed in the front matter of *Grad Study*. Then, before requesting application materials from particular programs, ask to speak with the faculty member who coordinates respecialization. He or she will likely interview you over the phone (especially if you're not local) or ask you to come in for an interview. Be prepared at the time you call to describe your credentials (both educational and career), to discuss why you are interested in respecializing, and to ask initial questions you may have about the program (e.g., Can you attend part-time? Is there a standard number of years you will have to attend? Is there standard coursework for everyone, or is each applicant's transcript and experience reviewed and coursework tailored accordingly? When and what kind of practicuum experiences will you participate in?). If you are qualified and if your goals are congruent with those of the program, you will be told what steps to take next. These steps will vary from program to program and are often quite different from those of the standard graduate application process (e.g., for respecialization students, deadlines may be different and standardized test scores are usually not required). Some of the advice we share in this book, however, can be useful if modified somewhat (e.g., if you are asked to write an essay describing your reasons for respecializing, you can modify our advice on application essays accordingly).

Additional Financial Aid Opportunities

Returning to our main discussion, in addition to writing to the psychology program regarding financial aid information, you should also call or write the financial aid office of the university and inquire about aid they administer to graduate students. Be sure to ask them if there are other sources of aid at the university you should contact for information, applications, and so on. Financial aid for graduate students may not be centralized or even coordinated (this differs from institution to institution). Some aid may be available through the psychology department and the specific program, some through the financial aid office, and some even through a third office, such as graduate affairs. The four basic categories of money available for graduate students (tuition remission; grants, fellowships, and scholarships; assistantships; and loans) may be administered differently at each university.

In the same vein, do not assume that information on financial aid received from one program will apply in any way to another program. As noted above, each institution administers financial aid somewhat differently. They also have different deadlines and may require different forms. Fortunately, however, many institutions use the same financial needs analysis forms (e.g., the GAPSFAS [Graduate and Professional School Financial Aid Services], FASA [Free Application for Federal Student Aid], and FAF [Financial Aid Form]).

While waiting for this information to arrive, we encourage you to look into other sources of financial aid. Most of the major publications on grants and other sources of financial aid for graduate students are too expensive to purchase, but they can be found in most university libraries or student services centers (see Resources). One notable exception is the affordable paperback book by Patricia McWade, *Financing Graduate School* (1993), which gives a good overview of the whole scheme of financial aid opportunities. In addition to aid from the federal government and private institutions, be sure to check the opportunities that states provide (keeping in mind residency requirements). Probably the best source of this information is the Office of Education in the state capital.

Students in certain categories will want to investigate additional sources of aid. The Office of Ethnic Minority Affairs of the APA offers a free publication, *Financial Aid Resources for Ethnic Minorities Pursuing Undergraduate, Graduate, and Post-Doctoral Study in Psychology*. Among the programs described is the Minority Fellowship Program (MFP; see Appendix E). Offering fellowships to students as well as technical assistance to professionals, the MFP is jointly funded by the APA and the National Institute of Mental Health and was established to improve and enlarge educational opportunities in psychology and neuroscience for ethnic minorities. In addition to providing fellowships, the MFP acts as an information clearinghouse and can provide a free list of organizations and contact names around the country that may offer financial aid to minority graduate students. Other major sources of aid for this population are the Dorothy Danforth Compton Minority Fellowship Program, the Ford Foundation Predoctoral and Dissertation Fellowships for Minorities, and the National Science Foundation Minority Graduate Fellowships (see Resources). Special financial aid opportunities for women, including women who are members of ethnic minorities, can be researched through *A Directory of Selected Scholarship, Fellowship, and Other Financial Aid Opportunities for Women and Ethnic Minorities in Psychology and Related Fields*, a free publication available through the APA's Women's Programs Office.

Organizing Incoming Material

When the information you have requested starts to arrive, you would be wise to invest in some file folders to store materials for each program, including your worksheets. Keep two files for each program, one for the admissions information and forms and the other for the financial aid data and forms. You still have a good bit of reading and research ahead of you, so file the materials as they arrive rather than waiting for them all to appear.

In response to your request for general information, most programs will send you at least two application forms, one for the university and one for the department or program. They will also send you informational brochures on the university in general, the program you're interested in, and financial aid and housing. The application forms themselves contain a wealth of procedural information. Program brochures typically include profiles of faculty members and a description of the training program and curriculum; occasionally, a program will supply you with some up-to-date statistics on former applicants, current enrollees, or graduates (e.g., academic qualifications or employment status).

Read the application forms and brochures thoroughly and record pertinent information on your program worksheets. Verify information that you had recorded from *Grad Study* (the information could have changed since your edition was published). Try to find answers to any questions you still have among the materials you have received.

Many programs will send you a list not only of faculty but also of their major areas of research and practice. Study this list to see if any (or several) faculty members share your interests, and also make note of those areas that you hadn't thought much about before but seem interesting to you as you read. Decide whether you would like to search *PsycLIT* or a similar database for publications by particular faculty members, and make a note in that regard. Note any pluses or minuses with regard to faculty interests on your program worksheet.

Highlight in some way those questions for which you still need information, but make sure you have read the program materials several times before doing so. Jot down any new questions that have occurred to you as you read program materials. Finally, summarize what you have learned about the program on your list of pros and cons.

When you receive the financial aid information, read every piece of paper you are sent carefully to determine deadlines for each and every form you must submit. Directors of financial aid have told us that missing initial deadlines is the number one mistake potential graduate students make. Write these deadlines on a piece of paper or note card and staple it to the front of the financial aid folder for every program.

Issues for Specific Populations

Members of specific populations often have additional questions at this time or wonder if there are questions they *should* be asking that haven't occurred to them. Minority students may want to know answers to the following questions, for example[3]:

- How many minorities students have been admitted to the program recently? How many finished their degrees? How does the retention rate for minorities compare with that for nonminorities?
- What percentage of full-time faculty are members of ethnic minorities? What percentage of tenured faculty? (Even if a member of a specific population does not want to specialize in serving or doing research about that population, the percentage of full-time faculty in their population may still be important in terms of the availability of same-sex or same-group mentors. In fact, mentorship was stressed by almost every woman and every member of ethnic minority groups that we spoke to while researching this book.)
- What kind of recruitment and retention strategies does the program use, in general and with regard to minority students in particular? What is the retention rate for minorities as compared with the majority student population?
- What kind of organizations are available for community and for support of students in general, minority students in particular?
- Are minority issues addressed in the curriculum? Is this done through a particular course or is information about minorities integrated throughout all or most courses?
- Is research about minorities valued and encouraged? Is there access to members of minority populations for such research? Is service to minorities possible during practica experiences? Internships? If such opportunities are limited at that program, is there an opportunity to network with faculty and students in other programs or at other universities?

Women and gay and lesbian individuals might have similar questions. For example, in addition to seeking information about female faculty, women may want to know if there is a women's studies program at the university and, if so, whether there is opportunity for interdisciplinary

---

3. We are thankful to Miguel Ybarra for providing these questions.

work. Is there a psychology of women course taught? Are women's issues considered throughout the curriculum? Are there opportunities for practica experiences and internships that focus particularly on women's issues (e.g., rape counseling, women's health care, domestic violence)? Other students may want to know if there are openly self-identified gay and lesbian students and faculty at the university and in the program. Are there student organizations for gay men and lesbians? Are the psychological aspects of being a gay or lesbian person included in the curriculum (e.g., in developmental psychology courses, in marital and family therapy courses?). Several excellent papers addressing gay and lesbian issues in the training of psychologists have been written, and these are listed in the Resources.

Obtaining Further Information

If you still have questions or need additional information, it is entirely appropriate to write to the program again, or even call. Any intelligent request is likely to be well-received, but if you are seeking information that is readily available in the materials sent to you, you will make a poor impression.

Who specifically should you call? Program directors are best prepared to answer questions about curricula as well as other general questions about the program. They will refer you to other individuals if necessary. Specific faculty members are best equipped to answer questions about their research and practice interests. Write down your questions in detail before making any calls. Again, if you have done your homework and are not asking for information already in the program materials, most faculty will find a direct and well-framed question or two quite appropriate.

It's natural to feel some anxiety in making such a personal contact, but at times it's the only way you can get the information you need. If you are calling with legitimate questions, your call is likely to be welcomed. But do not fish around for information about the best way to "get in," and do not try to "sell" your qualifications to any faculty member you speak with. This will not help you, and it might even hurt by creating a negative first impression. If someone is abrupt with you or acts as if your questions are inappropriate, try not to take it personally. Faculty members differ greatly in the availability of time they have to speak with potential graduate students. Don't rule out a program strictly on the basis of a curt or nonresponsive answer to your questions by one faculty member. That experience may not be at all representative of the general responsiveness of the faculty.

Students are perhaps the best resource for questions regarding the emotional atmosphere or "climate" of a program. Are faculty actively engaged with students or are they aloof or unapproachable? Are students treated respectfully? Are women and minorities treated as respectfully as White male students? Are students encouraged to be cooperative with their peers, or is there a feeling of cutthroat competition? Is mentorship encouraged? What happens if a student flounders in a particular course? Are there support groups for students in general or for members of specific populations in particular? Given the unavoidable rigor of psychology graduate programs, is the workload reasonable? Is there overt or subtle sexual harassment? Do gay and lesbian students typically feel safe enough in the program to be out? If students have dropped out of the program, why? A few general questions, such as how satisfied do students feel with their programs and why, can also be helpful.

How do you go about finding a student to respond to these questions? You can ask whoever answers the phone at the program's office whether there are any graduate students available to answer questions that applicants may have about graduate student life. If this person cannot direct you to someone, ask to speak to the director of the program or to a faculty member who could refer you to a student.

If you are unable to obtain the name of a student using this strategy, you may be able to network through the American Psychological Association of Graduate Students (APAGS; see Resources). As this book goes to press, APAGS is working out a system of state representatives. You can call the APAGS office to get the name and phone number of one of their members-at-large. They may be able to direct you to students in the states in which your programs are located who might be able to answer your questions regarding the emotional climate of programs, as well as other questions you may have.

As you get answers to your questions, some programs will seem more attractive than before, and others may be eliminated from your list altogether. Be aware that you are not likely to get answers to all of your questions. You should be tenacious, however, in gathering the information that is most important to you. It will be difficult to compare programs if vital information is absent for some programs.

Step 5.6: Compile a Final List of Programs That You Will Apply To

Your current list of possibilities is likely to be somewhat smaller than your earlier, preliminary list. As you obtained more information, you may have decided against some programs. The information before you now should enable you to narrow your list even further so that it includes only the programs that you will actually apply to.

How do you do this? In step 5.4, before you had contacted programs for additional information, we instructed you to categorize programs as strong bets, good bets, and long shots and to discard improbable selections. To make your final selections, you should do the same thing once again. Knowing everything you now know about the programs and what they are looking for in candidates, sort through them and make sure they are still in the proper categories. As a practical strategy, if you have file folders for each program, put them in three piles to represent the three categories: good bets, strong bets, and long shots (any improbables will not have been retained).

Then comes the truly hard part. Within each category, look at each program carefully, particularly with regard to those training requirements and program preferences that are most important to you. Begin to rank order the programs in order of your preference, with the highest ranked program at the top of the pile. Note any "ties" that occur.

How many programs should be on your final list? Ten is a number often recommended. However, if you are applying to a program that offers training in a highly popular specialty or area of concentration (e.g., a clinical program housed in a university psychology department), you may want to apply to a few more. You are free to apply to as many programs as you wish, but applying to a large number of programs is not very practical, and we do not recommend it. There is no evidence to suggest that your chances for acceptance increase in direct proportion to the number of applications you submit. Also, there is considerable time and money associated with each application you submit. It can take several weeks to assemble everything you need to submit an application, and for each one you must pay application fees and fees for transcripts and test reports, not to mention postage. As we mentioned earlier, you can safely estimate a minimum expenditure of $40 per application. Moreover, if you have researched programs thoroughly, you should be able to identify the 10 or so that match your needs and qualifications best.

Among your final selections you should concentrate on applying primarily to good bets (possibly 5 out of your 10 final selections). So, take the first five programs in the good-bets category. You should also apply to several programs that you are amply qualified for (strong bets), so pick the top three in that category. If there are one or two programs that you are extremely interested in but seem like long shots to you, select them as well. You will have to work harder to present yourself as a viable candidate for these programs, but the effort could pay off.

If you are having difficulty evaluating all of the information you have, here is some general advice that may help you make your final determinations. If you have more than 15 good matches before you, take a closer look at the relative attractiveness of programs by comparing them in pairs within each category (i.e., strong bets, good bets, and long shots). For programs that appear to offer equally suitable training, look again at general measures of quality (see Table 5.1). You may be able to discriminate between two programs of equal quality on the basis of some feature that has gained increasing importance to you as you have had time to mull over the results of your research.

If you still have too many programs on your list that seem equally desirable, listen to your gut-level reactions. All other things being equal, select the programs that made the best impression on you or that appealed to you strongly, even if you can't define the particular reason.

Step 5.7: Visit the Programs on Your Final List (Optional)

Ideally, you would visit every school to which you will apply. Practically, however, many if not most students are unable to afford the time off from work or school or the considerable expense such travel involves. Moreover, if your budget is limited (and most applicants' are), it is more important to set aside money to attend preselection interviews, which may have a direct bearing on whether you are accepted by a program (see chapter 7).

However, for members of certain groups, an earlier visit might be invaluable. Gay and lesbian applicants and members of minority groups, in particular, may learn how welcome they are likely to feel only by visiting the campus. Students with disabilities usually need first-hand knowledge of how accessible a campus and a community are.

If you do have the time and money to visit some or all of the schools you've decided to apply to, by all means do. A great deal can be learned from visits, especially if you are able to talk with current graduate students. You may be able to get answers to some lingering questions. And, not to be facetious (or unscientific), there is one thing you can explore only by being there: vibes! You might be spending a good deal of time in this place and with these people, so it's always helpful to get a feel for the place and for how well you would fit in.

The best time for an informational visit is in the early fall—before you apply and before staff and faculty are totally preoccupied with the business of the fall semester. We advise you not to just drop in, but to write to the program or call ahead. Ask if there is someone on campus who can arrange a time at which you can have a tour of the grounds and facilities and if there are any graduate students or faculty who could meet briefly with you.

It may be possible for you to obtain an interview with a particular faculty member; however, this is a somewhat delicate matter, and programs have different policies regarding this practice. Many do not interview with students unless they have been selected as finalists. So first ask program staff what their policy is, and determine whether your request would be welcomed. If there is no objection, ask if you should contact the faculty person yourself. If you sense any hesitance, you should not pursue an interview with a particular faculty member. If you decide to go ahead and request an interview, make sure that you have a legitimate reason, such as a need for specialized information that is not accessible from printed materials or program staff or that cannot be handled as well by phone. If you plan to undertake a very particular kind of study that falls under a particular faculty member's area of expertise, your need to explore possibilities directly with the person who would be likely to oversee your work may be considered a legitimate reason for an interview. Finally, if you do obtain an interview with any faculty member, conduct yourself with utmost professionalism (see chapter 7 for a discussion of preselection interviews). Before you meet, reread everything that you have received about the program, so that you ask intelligent questions that are not already answered in these materials. Again, do not try to "sell" yourself to any faculty member. This is not the purpose of the visit.

In general, be aware that many programs may not have the resources to show you around campus or to have you interview any faculty at this point. It may count against you in the long run if you are demanding in this regard. You shouldn't hold it against a program if they do not have the resources for a personalized visit. They may have several hundred applicants each year, and they couldn't possibly arrange visits for even a fraction of them and still do their jobs with their enrolled students.

An alternative to contacting faculty regarding a visit is to find out if there's a chapter of Psi Chi (the national honor society in psychology) on campus or an APAGS representative and, if there is, to contact them. They may be able to arrange for you to visit and talk with students (particularly graduate students) who are familiar with the faculty and the program.

Conclusion

You have now completed one of the most time-consuming tasks in the application process, a task that many applicants shortchange in their haste to fill out applications and get them in the mail. As a result of your hard work, you have an edge over your competition in several ways. First, you have the confidence of knowing that the decisions you have made are based on a rational process rather than on impulsivity. Second, you know well the programs you have selected, and you know how and why they are a good match for you. Therefore, when you ask for letters of recommendation and begin writing your personal essays, you will be coming from a position of strength. Finally, and perhaps most important, those programs that accept you will be programs in which you will be most likely to succeed, because they are all good matches in terms of philosophy, goals, and the means of achieving them.

Applying to Graduate Programs

To tend, unfailingly, unflinchingly, towards a goal is the secret of success.—*Anna Pavlova*

Your ultimate goal is to gain admission to one or more of the graduate psychology programs you have selected. However, that is a decision over which you do not have complete control. A related goal that you do have control over is the quality of your applications. In this chapter, we describe how to prepare your applications in a way that boosts your chances for success. Our intent is to simplify the procedure for you as much as possible. Your task is to pay scrupulous attention to every detail every step of the way. We recommend that you be obsessive in this task, double-checking everything periodically to make sure that you haven't overlooked any minor (but perhaps crucial) detail.

Getting Ready

Before you begin, you will want to first obtain supplies and get organized. Useful supplies to have include high-quality white bond paper, a typewriter and new ribbon (for the application and financial aid forms), word processing equipment (for the essays), a fine-point black pen, your applicant worksheet, all program worksheets and program and financial aid file folders, blank postcards, envelopes (9″ × 12″ for your applications; letter-sized for faculty letters of recommendation), and postage stamps. You should also make one photocopy of all blank application and financial aid forms. You will be writing your first draft on the photocopy and then typing the final on the original form.

Because you are going to be generating a lot of paperwork, it's a good idea to devise an efficient method for tracking it. One suggestion is an application checklist, such as the one presented in Exhibit 6.1. Using this checklist, you can record and see at a glance when application ele-

Exhibit 6.1

Application Checklist

Program Name _____

Application Deadline _____ Financial Aid Deadline _____

Application Elements	Date Requested	Date Received
Transcripts		
_____	_____	_____
_____	_____	_____
_____	_____	_____
GRE-General Scores	_____	_____
GRE-Psychology Scores	_____	_____
MAT Scores	_____	_____
Letters of Recommendation		
_____	_____	_____
_____	_____	_____
_____	_____	_____
Program Application Packet	_____	_____
Financial Aid Packet	_____	_____
Additional Notes:		

ments have been completed, sent, and confirmed for each program on your final list. You can staple the checklist on either the outside or the inside of each folder.

Arrange your application and financial aid materials in order of earliest to latest application and financial aid deadlines. You will complete applications for those programs with the earliest deadlines first, even though some of the first steps will involve all programs (i.e., all transcripts, test scores, and letters of recommendation will be requested at the same time). You may want to purchase a calendar that can serve as a master schedule for all of your deadlines, including dates by which materials should have been received by your programs. When you see all your deadlines in black and white, you can then plan your own interim deadlines for particular application elements (e.g., first draft of essays for first three programs ready for review November 1; revised essays completed November 15). These interim deadlines are important because you don't want to overschedule yourself on particular weeks (i.e., writing 10 essays in one week). Checking your master calendar daily and weekly, modifying it as necessary, will help you keep on track.

Ideally, you will begin preparing applications no later than 2 months before the earliest deadline of the programs you are applying to and the financial aid you are asking for. If you can begin earlier than that, by all means do.

Remember to maintain thorough records of everything you send. Keep photocopies of requests for transcripts and score reports; letters of recommendation; correspondence; postage receipts; and the complete set of application materials that you send to each program. If anything is lost, you will save yourself the trouble of having to redo everything from scratch. Record the dates of all transactions on your application checklist (e.g., when you mailed each transcript request and when you verified it was received). You can help ensure being notified when some materials have been received by including, when appropriate, a self-addressed, stamped postcard with your application materials, such as with your letters of recommendation. Keep track of estimated receipt times, and follow up on any materials that appear to have been delayed.

Finally, be compulsively neat and careful. The physical appearance of your materials will create an important first impression. Whenever possible, use a typewriter or word processor, but do not use italics or decorative fonts. Always have someone else proofread your materials for typographical errors, after you have done so. A fresh eye can pick up errors that you, because you have been immersed in the process, may not. Double-check every piece of paper in your application packet before you mail it, making sure that all materials are complete and are going to the right programs.

Step 6.1: Request Transcripts and Test Score Reports

You will need to allow approximately 6 weeks for both transcripts and standardized test reports to be received by your programs. So, if your earliest program deadline is January 1 and it is November 1 already, you need to take this step immediately. If your deadlines are later, you may want to get started on other steps that are more time consuming. Just be sure to request transcripts in time for them to be received by the program that has the earliest application deadline.

It makes little difference whether you request transcripts or test scores first, but it is more expedient to process all transcript requests at the same time and all score report requests at the same time. To begin, reread each program's instructions in its application packet as to how many transcripts and which test reports are required, and record these on your checklist. Call your undergraduate institution (or institutions, if you attended more than one) and ask their procedures for obtaining transcripts. Some schools will send you a form to fill out and others will request a simple letter, signed in ink, requesting transcripts and providing the exact mailing information for the institutions to which they should be sent (universities should send official transcripts to your programs, not directly to you). Be sure to verify the amount of money you will need to send for *each* transcript. Follow these procedures to the letter. Request transcripts for each undergraduate institution you attended and for each of the programs you are applying to, and order an extra copy from each institution for yourself. You can use this copy to generate photocopies for your recommenders. And, if you want to really be on the safe side, send a photocopy of both transcripts and standardized test scores with your application, noting that official copies have been requested. That way, even if official copies are late, many programs may still consider your application. If you are a first-semester senior, be aware that you may have to send a second transcript later when your fall grades have been recorded. Check your application instructions for each school to see if this is the case. If so, be sure to put this on your checklist and your master deadline schedule. Finally, make sure that you enclose enough money to cover fees for sending each transcript. Requests that are not accompanied by the correct amount of money may not be processed at all. Photocopy both the request and the check.

Testing agencies allow you to order a number of score reports on your test registration form (up to four for the GRE and up to three for the MAT). So, if you had made your final program choices by the time you registered for the tests, some of your test scores may already have been reported (but be sure to double-check this). For the remainder, test bulletins contain forms for requesting additional reports, or you can request a form from the testing agency. Again, enclose the fee that may be required and be sure to make photocopies of your requests and to record the date you made the request on your application checklist for each program.

As far as follow-up is concerned, some programs will alert you if transcripts and test reports have or have not been received. However, you should assume ultimate responsibility for ensuring that transcripts and test reports have been received on time (see step 6.7).

Step 6.2: Prepare a Resume

As we stated in chapter 4, a resume is not usually required for application; therefore, if you are extremely pressed for time, you can skip this step. However, if time permits, we recommend doing one for three reasons. First, resumes are very useful to people who write letters of recommendation. They give the recommender a more complete picture of your abilities and achievements than they may have had in their interactions with you. They provide the recommender with specific supporting evidence of claims he or she may make. Resumes also jog recommenders' memories about aspects they may have forgotten, and they serve to stress the kinds of information you want to be emphasized in your letter. Second, in one survey of doctoral psychology programs, resumes were frequently recommended as a strategy for enhancing the application (Eddy, Lloyd, & Lubin, 1987). Such resumes often provide information not available through the other application elements. Resumes can be particularly important for returning students, who may have a number of years of solid experience, representing not only skills and aptitudes but also evidence of commitment, maturity, and professionalism. These students should devote considerable time and care in showcasing their finest attributes and achievements through a resume. Finally, because you will summarize job and education chronology on your resume, it will be a handy reference to have when you fill out the application forms for each program. There is one caveat to this advice: If, when you draft your resume, you find that you have little to record (see later discussion), you may decide that such a sparse resume may leave a negative impression. In that case, don't send it in with your application materials.

If you decide to do a resume, the best time to do so is before you ask people to write letters of recommendation. Even if you have a current resume you have used in a job search, you will need to tailor it for this purpose. When you list your jobs, for example, you should provide minimal information about those jobs that are unrelated to academic skills or to psychology. You should emphasize any skills used on a job that would be pertinent to academic prowess or to success as a psychologist. For example, your job frying burgers at a fast-food restaurant would be downplayed or even omitted, but your duties collecting data for an insurance company would be highlighted.

Your resume should not be longer than two pages, and one page is ideal. Headings should reinforce those aspects of your experience most pertinent to being a psychology student or a future psychologist. These might include career objectives, education, papers presented at professional associations, papers published, honors, research experience, teaching experience, clinical experience, psychology-related field experiences, professional affiliations (especially any offices you held), and job experience. If you were supervised by a doctoral-level individual in any activities, you might include that in your description. You might also include interests, if you think these would contribute to your being viewed as a well-rounded yet professional individual.

There are a number of published resources, workshops, and even computer software to assist you in styling your resume (i.e., choosing the format). Any number of styles are satisfactory, as long as the resume is easy to read and the effect is professional. For additional information, consult a librarian or browse at your local bookstore. For personalized help, see whether the career counseling office on your campus or a county department of adult education has individual or group workshops on preparing an effective resume.

Step 6.3: Request Letters of Recommendation

In chapter 4, we discussed the importance of letters of recommendation and offered some advice on choosing sources. (Before you choose and approach potential recommenders, you may want to review that discussion.) Basically, letters of recommendation give the program an outside perspective on your abilities and potential that will help them further clarify the picture they have of you. When candidates are otherwise matched on objective criteria, the quality of their letters of recommendation can determine which of them are ultimately selected.

What makes for a high-quality letter? First, it is written by someone who knows about the abilities needed to be successful in graduate school and as a psychologist. He or she knows you well enough to make an informed judgment about you with regard to the qualities that make for success and to back up these judgments with supporting details. A recommender should be able to write about your general intelligence, ability to analyze and synthesize data and concepts, goal-oriented thinking or problem-solving abilities, oral and written communication skills, motivation, tenacity, work habits, study-related skills, maturity, and leadership potential. He or she should be able to identify your strengths and to compare you favorably with successful graduate students they have worked with in the past. As an added plus (but not a necessity), the recommender might be familiar with the particular program to which you are applying (Eddy et al., 1987) and be able to evaluate the match between your goals and the focus of the program. Perhaps most important, the recommender should have a highly positive view of you that will be conveyed between the lines.

Application instructions will stipulate how many letters are required (three is standard) and from whom. Most programs will either send you a form (see example in Appendix D) or provide printed instructions for the recommender to follow. A few programs may simply request a certain number of letters of recommendation, without instructions or specification of content.

You should already have received forms or instructions in your application packet for each program. This packet should also explain how the letters should be sent. For example, some schools ask the recommender to send the letter directly to them. Other schools prefer that the student collect the letters and mail them in together. For every school you will apply to, list on your application checklist, under "Additional Notes," the number and type of recommendations required, to whom and how they should be sent, and the deadline for receipt. You will want to send only the number and kind of letters requested to each school in the way the school wants them to be sent!

If you have followed our advice, you will have given some thought earlier to potential sources of recommendations and listed some names on your applicant worksheet. Now is the time to choose among them. In chapter 4, we described the ideal recommender as a professor of one or more rigorous psychology courses you have taken, with whom you have done research or an independent study and who knows you well academically and perhaps personally. The closer the person fits this description, the more credibility he or she is likely to have. Most recommenders will only fit part of that bill, but if you can assemble a *package* of letters that covers all of the above bases, then you will still be in good stead. If you cannot obtain all of your letters from psychology professors, the best alternatives are professors of math, other sciences, or composition courses and supervisors of psychology-related field or work experiences. Other things being equal, choose the person who is the most familiar with you and the one who has given you detailed, mostly positive feedback on your work in the past (e.g., on essay exams or class papers). Again, it is not one letter but the package of letters that you should be most concerned with. Rank the names you have selected.

Once you have chosen your final list of potential recommenders, you must approach each one, starting with the one at the top of your list, and ask if they are willing to write a letter. Most recommenders prefer at least three or four weeks to write, type, and mail a set of letters. If you need the letter sooner, sometimes a recommender will agree, but it's really to your advantage to give your recommender enough time to do a good job. When you approach them, it's better to call and schedule an appointment than to make your request on the phone. (If you are still in school, you might stop by, but only during office hours. If you are an employee, choose a time when your supervisor is not under a lot of stress to request some time to talk.) A personal encounter gives your potential recommenders the opportunity to ask you questions that will assist them in deciding whether to grant your request and that will aid them in writing good letters if they do agree. However, if your recommenders are a considerable distance away, you will have to call them and then follow up that call with a letter.

Recommenders are likely to be writing letters for several students, and in addition to knowing your deadlines, they also need to know when you will be providing supporting materials so that they can plan their time accordingly. When you meet with your recommender, let them know when you will be providing the following information:

- the recommendation form (or forms) and instructions that were supplied with each program's application, on which you have typed in your name and indicated whether you waive your right to review the form[1];
- your resume (make sure you include a phone number where you can be reached);

---

1. The Privacy Act of 1974 ensures that you can see the contents of your files, which would include letters such as these. If you have selected your recommenders carefully, you don't really need to see the letters. Recommenders may appreciate the trust you invest in them, and the program may assume that the letter is more candid if you have waived that right. But if you feel strongly that you would like to review the letters, then do not waive this right.

- a copy of your transcript and standardized test scores, if available;
- stamped envelopes addressed to each program the recommender is to send letters to; and
- self-addressed, stamped postcards to be sent to each program with instructions to the program to return the card to you upon receipt of the letter of recommendation (it could simply say, "This acknowledges receipt of letter from [fill in name of recommender] to [fill in name of university and program]").

Make sure that you photocopy blank forms and instructions, in case your recommender misplaces them. If you think a particular paper or exam you wrote while in their class (or one that you presented during a professional meeting or published) would be helpful in their assessment, include it in your information packet.

Sometimes there are no forms or instructions. If your recommender is a psychology professor, he or she should be quite familiar with the kind of information that is appropriate. Other recommenders may need more guidance. For example, an English professor might need to be briefed on the kinds of abilities psychology graduate programs are looking for. Recommenders who are not teachers may need even more guidance. For them, you should summarize the categories of evaluation that would likely be useful to the program (see earlier discussion; you might want to summarize or photocopy relevant information from this step and from the discussion in chapter 4). If any of your recommenders have not written such letters before, you may want to suggest that they be specific and that they quantify and support their general claims with concrete details, if possible (e.g., you're not just a good writer; instead, you are "one of the top five writers this teacher has ever taught. Her review of the literature on _____ was one of the best student papers I've ever read."). If no length is specified by the program, you might want to suggest a maximum of two single-spaced pages. Finally, before you meet your recommenders, on the front of their information packets write the number of letters to be sent, the date the earliest letter is due, and to whom each is to be sent.

What should you say when you meet? Rather than simply asking for a letter, you might first state your rationale for selecting your recommender. This will remind them that they think well of you and that they have concrete reasons for that assessment. For example, you might say, "I thought you'd be an appropriate person to ask because you know of my _____ (list one or more abilities or activities, e.g., outstanding paper, diligence in research, leadership in class discussions, etc.). You're also knowledgeable about the kind of applicants that graduate schools are looking for, such as _____ (list the most important things you would like the recommender to emphasize). Do you feel you know me well enough to write such a letter?"

If the person shows any hesitance, do not try to persuade them otherwise. They may actually be too busy to write a quality letter, they may know they're not very good at it, or they may not be able to write a wholeheartedly positive letter about you. In any case, be polite and thank them for their time. Then go back to your list and select another name.

If the person is willing and able to write a letter, be sure to request all of the letters you need at once (you may be asking them to send forms or letters to 10 programs, not just 1, even though they all may be similar). You will want to reiterate the information you have written on the front of the packet, tactfully stressing when the earliest deadline is. If a recommender is notorious for being late, you may want to give a deadline of a week or two earlier than the actual deadline. Be sure to explain what you have included in the packet. If they are mailing their letters directly to the program, ask them to include the appropriate postcard from the packet. Finally, make sure you thank the recommender explicitly. Letters of recommendation take considerable time and creative energy, and this effort should be acknowledged.

If it is impossible for you to appear in person to make your request, you should discuss in a telephone call the same things you would in a meeting. If it has been some time since you've met, first remind the recommender of who you are (e.g., "In the fall of 1992 I took your course in experimental psychology and assisted in your research on _____ .") and explain your purpose fully. You might also brief them about what you have been doing academically and professionally since the time you were acquainted. If the person agrees to write your letter, send them your information packet, with a cover letter again reminding them of the context in which they knew you, summarizing what you have enclosed, and reiterating the deadlines. Encourage your recommender to contact you by phone if he or she needs further information about you.

Be sure to write on your master calendar the date you expect to receive a postcard verifying the letter has been received. If you do not receive one, call the program to check. If one of your letters has failed to arrive on time, you should contact your recommender and tactfully inquire about your letter. You might say something to the effect of "I've just learned from my program(s) that all of my letters of recommendation have not been received. Can you tell me when you sent yours?" If the person says the letter was sent, ask if you can pick up a photocopy to resend, because you fear the original has been lost somewhere in the mail. If the person tells you they've been remiss in writing it, ask if they could write it now and perhaps you could mail it overnight express (that is, if you're that close to the deadline). If they need time beyond the deadline but you believe they will write a good letter, one option would be to call the program and ask if the deadline can be extended for that single item. If not, you may have to scurry around to find another recommender who can write a letter immediately. This situation is one of the stickiest in the application process, and it raises the anxiety of most applicants considerably. Be vigilant about the deadlines, and do the best you can to rectify problems if they arise.

Step 6.4: Write Application Essays

We suggest that you work on the next three steps concurrently, that is, that you alternate between drafting versions of your application essays and filling in your financial aid and application forms. The process of writing essays, reviewing them, getting feedback, and revising the essays accordingly requires concentration, imagination, and time lags between versions. Filling out forms periodically will provide a welcome respite from this intense creative process. Order your essay questions from earliest to latest deadline and begin with the earliest one.

As you will see in the discussion that follows, we suggest that you devote considerable time and effort to these essays. This is because, like letters of recommendation, essays are often used to make final selections of students with similar GPAs and standardized test scores. If you are on the borderline of being accepted and the admissions committee could go either way, a sterling essay can increase your chances of success considerably. Remember also that essays give you a chance to express yourself in ways that are not possible on the application form itself. That is, you have an opportunity to elaborate on your interests and qualifications, express your enthusiasm for psychology, and explain why you are uniquely suitable for admission to a particular program.

In chapter 4, we summarized the kinds of essays often requested by programs. The three most typical themes include your long-term career plans, your areas of interest in academic psychology, and your reasons for choosing the program. But by now you have received the exact assignments from your application materials. A few of the programs you chose may have asked for an almost identical essay, and there is likely to be *some* overlap in the categories of information requested by many of the programs. Most will differ on at least one dimension, however, and you must be prepared to write an original essay for every program on your list. Even those that request the exact same information may need to be tailored if you discuss the match between yourself and the particular program. Most programs will specify the length of the essay (many are 500 words or two double-spaced pages). Your essay should never be longer than is requested and should come as close as possible to the word limit specified. The same is true of the content specifications. If they ask for a career goal statement, focus on describing your career goals, not your family history. If they ask you to describe why you are applying to their program, focus on what you know about the program and why you believe it is a good match for you. If you are asked to submit a one-page, double-spaced, and typed essay, do not submit a two-page, single-spaced, handwritten essay! So, your first priority should be to respond appropriately to what is asked of you. If no length is specified, we suggest that you keep your essay between 500 and 1,000 words. Anything longer may be considered a burden by the busy admissions committee members who have to read them.

If you are asked to write an "autobiographical essay" or given an open-ended assignment, such as "tell us something about you," your first reaction may be to feel even more overwhelmed. Summing up your life in a page or two can be quite daunting, and trying to tell a program "something" may leave you up in the air. We suggest that you focus on summarizing significant experiences or events that helped to shape you as a person and influenced your present goals and ambitions. It will also generally be in your interest to reveal in your essay the relationship between your career goals and academic interests, on the one hand, and the program's focus and philosophy, on the other. In that way you can demonstrate not only that you have given considerable thought to what you intend to do with your degree, but also that you have taken care to find a program that has the faculty, resources, and kinds of training that are compatible with your goals.

Gay and lesbian applicants often wonder if they should be open about their sexual orientation in their personal essay. This decision must be made on a case-by-case basis and involves both practical and philosophical issues. As a practical concern, for example, if someone has psychology-related experience (e.g., has done research or counseling) with the gay population and such experience would be an asset on an application, it may make sense to include that experience and thus indirectly self-disclose. If the person wants to do research or provide services to gay/lesbian clients as a primary focus of their graduate program, they may also want to self-identify. If sexual orientation is irrelevant to past psychology-related experience and future aspirations, a student may opt not to reveal that he or she is gay on the application. Philosophically, one of a student's strong values may be openness with regard to sexual orientation, and this value may override caution with regard to self-identifying. Others may value such openness only with people they have come to know and consider this private information not to be generally shared. Again, it must be decided by the student on a case-by-case basis. There is no right or wrong answer.

Members of other specific populations who wonder whether they should make a point of their group status might apply the above reasoning as well. In general, the more relevant your group status is to your qualifications or academic and career aspirations, the more appropriate it would be to mention this in an application essay.

To the extent possible, use the essay as an opportunity to highlight your uniqueness and your strengths. To cite but one example, the single, one-month volunteer work experience you listed on your application may not look as impressive as it really is. You may be able to elaborate on the experience in an essay to provide details such as you worked 40 hours a week; you became your supervisor's most valued assistant, accompanying him or her on data collection excursions in the field; you learned to use special lab equipment; or you got authorship credit for helping to write a final report. It could well be that this experience was highly influential to your decision to pursue a career in psychology. Peruse your applicant and program worksheets and resume to find relevant information that could be highlighted in your essay.

The most common problem students have in this step is not allowing sufficient time for developing their essays. In the best of all possible worlds, when you received your application packets you reviewed the essay requirements and allowed your ideas to germinate as you went ahead with other steps in the process. If you did that, you're ahead of the game. In any case, you need to allow sufficient time to brainstorm, write a first draft, revise it, get feedback, revise it again (and perhaps again), type it, and proofread it carefully. If there are 10 programs on your list, you can see why you should start on this step immediately.

Which may bring you to the second most common problem applicants have: writer's block. Simply looking at a white sheet of paper with

Exhibit 6.2

Tips on Writing Essays

- Allow yourself ample time to write, revise, edit, and proofread.
- Be willing to write as many drafts as are necessary to produce a unified, coherent essay.
- Attend to the instructions carefully to discern what the program is most interested in knowing about you.
- Follow instructions to the letter; adhere to length limitations, and answer everything that is asked.
- Don't repeat data that are already in your application, such as standardized test scores or GPAs.
- To the extent possible, use the essay as an opportunity to highlight your uniqueness and your strengths.
- Describe yourself honestly and realistically; acknowledge your weak points (if requested) and stress your good points without exaggerating. Try to connect the latter with your aspirations in psychology.
- Emphasize material that makes you appropriately different from other candidates or that gives you a special perspective (you may be unique in that you are one of the best limbo dancers in the Caribbean, but that would not be appropriate for this sort of essay).
- Demonstrate that you have taken the time to familiarize yourself with the program. Emphasize the match between your goals and those of the program.
- Use formal English and strike a serious tone; avoid slang, cliches, and jocularity. Pay attention to grammar and spelling. Mistakes in these areas can significantly detract from your essay's message.
- Don't feel you must dress up your essay with big words and with jargon. It's the "right" word, not the complex word, that counts. Jargon is tricky. If you misuse it, you create a negative impression that is difficult to erase.
- Watch out for superlative language, such as "all," "every," "always," and "never," unless it's clearly and unequivocally true.
- Read your essay out loud to identify trouble spots.
- Have someone else help edit and proofread your work. A person with good writing skills could help you with style, grammar, and spelling; a psychology professor could assist you with content and tone.

a question printed at the top may cause immediate paralysis of cognitive and verbal faculties. You feel convinced that you don't know *what* to say and certain that you don't know *how* to say it. You are not alone. Even applicants who aced their writing assignments in college, or workers whose jobs frequently require writing, freeze at this point.

In such situations, many writers have found it useful to divide the essay project into five phases: clustering, freewriting, revising, obtaining feedback, and revising again. The first phase, clustering, is a brainstorming technique popularized by Gabriele Rico (1983), a professor of English. The remainder of the phases described here are guided by principles developed by Peter Elbow (1981), also a college-level writing instructor, so we will briefly review their techniques. However, if you find them useful and want more detail, we have listed their books in the resource list. If you have your own favorite ways of freeing yourself from writer's block, by all means use them. For those of you who do not, you might want to give the techniques below a try. (For readers with their own methods who will skip the following discussion, we have summarized some pointers to keep in mind in Exhibit 6.2; these readers may also want to read the discussion on revising presented later in this step.)

Clustering

According to Rico (1983), clustering is useful whenever you don't know what to write about with regard to a specific topic. To understand how it works, take one of your essay questions and follow these instructions. First, summarize the question into one to three words. For example, if the question is "Why did you select the counseling program at _____ University?" you would write in the center of the cluster, "why this program." If they ask you to respond to more than one question, find a couple of words for each. For example, if you are asked to "describe your academic interests and the career you hope to be prepared for," you would write "academic interests" and "career plans." These will be your "nucleus" words. Then, take an unlined sheet of paper for *each* question, put the nucleus word or words in the upper third of the page, and circle them.

You are now ready to brainstorm. Set aside at least 10 minutes of uninterrupted quiet time. Look at the words in the center and write down in a word or two any associations or connections that come to you. Write them in such a way that they radiate outward from the nucleus word (see Figure 6.1). If you have trouble thinking of any, consider using the following categories as springboards for your thoughts: your strengths, accomplishments, needs, background, experiences, incidents, abilities, skills, interests, ideals, character, expectations, goals, plans, and ways of looking at the world. If you are focusing on the program, you might consider the program's assets, faculty, uniqueness, scope, and philosophy. Be specific as you marshal as many arguments as you can make for admission to a particular program. Having actively assessed your qualifications in chapter 4 and having thoroughly researched your programs in chapter 5, you will be way ahead of the candidate who simply plunges into the application process.

Figure 6.1

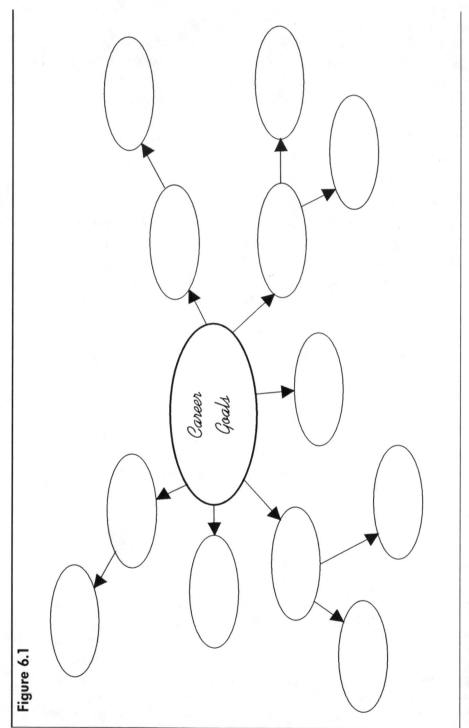

Sample blank cluster for a career goal essay.

Figure 6.2

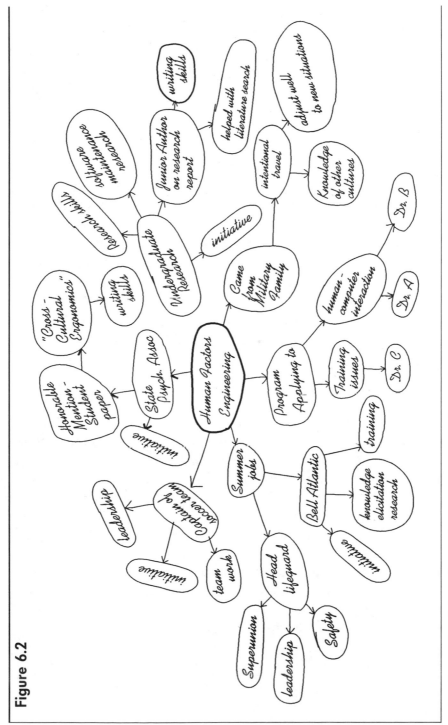

Sample completed cluster for applying to a program in human factors engineering.

As you write down specific words related to these or other categories, don't edit or censor anything. Put down *any* associations, no matter how minor or silly they might seem at this time. These will be your secondary words. After you have written down all your associations to the nucleus word, write down associations to your secondary words, and so on (see Figure 6.2). When you can't think of anything else, quit.

Now look at your cluster. Is there a theme or a pattern that emerges? If not, don't worry. If one doesn't emerge now, it will when you get to the next phase. If you see one or more themes or patterns, jot them down at the top of the page. Next, look at the elements of your cluster again. Darken the circles around those that seem most important to your theme. If you don't yet have a theme, put yourself in the place of your audience. If you were a faculty member, your task would be to read dozens of these essays and choose from among them the students you would most want to teach in the future. What elements in this cluster would be of most interest to you? Darken the circles around those elements. (Do not throw away these clusters, even after you have written your essays. They may be useful when you are preparing for possible preselection interviews [see chapter 7].)

Freewriting

Your next step is to freewrite. According to Elbow (1981), freewriting is a technique that liberates even the most blocked writer. First, allow at least 20 minutes of uninterrupted quiet time. Then, with your cluster in front of you, simply begin to write, putting into sentences elements from your cluster and providing supportive detail, particularly concrete examples or illustrative incidents. As Elbow suggests, don't try to organize it or worry how to start it. Just get sentences on paper without stopping. Keep the pen or keyboard moving. If you don't know what to write at a certain point, write "I don't know what else to write," but keep moving. Don't evaluate what you are writing. Don't read it over and cross out words or sentences. Your goal at this point is not logical, clear expression but simply getting ideas down on paper. You will worry about the rest when we get to the next phase. Stop at the end of 20 minutes, unless you have some additional points that you still want to add.

When you are finished, take a break. You may want to fill out some forms (see steps 6.4 and 6.5) or do something different altogether. Later in the day or tomorrow, when you're feeling fresh again, you will start revising.

Revising

Revising is something you will do several times: at least once or twice now and then once again after you have gotten feedback on your essay from others. Your goals in these revisions include (a) finding a theme or focus for your essay, (b) developing a logical order of paragraphs and sentences within paragraphs, (c) making the essay come alive with detail and language, (d) writing an expanded first draft, (e) cutting that draft down to size, and (f) creating an attention-grabbing lead sentence. Accomplishing these goals may take several work sessions.

To begin, get out your cluster and your freewriting. Consider your freewriting first. Has a theme or focus emerged? Look carefully to see if you can discern a pattern. It doesn't have to be unusual. For example, the hypothetical student whose cluster was presented in Exhibit 6.2 might decide that his research experiences as an undergraduate and his summer job at Bell Atlantic were crucial to his decision to become a psychologist concentrating on human factors engineering and that in both of these instances he displayed a lot of initiative. Using this as his theme, he would then weave in other experiences from his cluster that support what he is saying about himself and his interests in psychology. Again, the most successful essays are those that are built around a central point, even if that point is not dramatic. If you're stuck thinking of your own theme, move on to the next step, ordering, which may help clarify your focus.

To order your material you may want to cut and paste your freewriting or you may want to use an outline. Some people combine both: They sketch an outline and then cut up their material and place it under the appropriate heading in the outline. You're still not concerned about wording yet. You simply want to get things in some logical order. There are several typical orderings. As you may remember from freshman composition, you can argue inductively or deductively. Inductive reasoning starts from specific instances and leads toward a conclusion. For example, you could describe two or three instances of something (e.g., experience, attribute, skill) and then explain what they have in common. Deductive reasoning starts with a generalization and then confirms it with facts.

Once you have your headings or groupings, see if together they lead to a general conclusion—something that could be your organizing theme. Because a central focus or theme is so important, if you don't have one yet, you may have to backtrack to your cluster and add new elements until a theme emerges. Don't think that the theme has to be earth-shattering or even highly significant. Selection committees do not expect you to have a sophisticated philosophy based on worlds of knowledge and experience; they are more interested in your abilities, in your potential, and in the nature and degree of your interest in psychology. Again, they are asking themselves the question, Is this a person I would like to teach? Faculty are typically overworked. Your ability to focus your thoughts will make their job much easier, and this in itself will be counted in your favor.

Once you have a theme and a reasonable order to your essay, begin to expand your ideas, using brief concrete examples and illustrations if possible. Be specific, not vague. One possibility is to search for an incident related to your theme that illustrates the point you're making. And don't just describe your background—interpret it, give it meaning. For example, how exactly did being in a military family affect your interest in psychology? You want your audience to get a sense of a flesh-and-blood person with real-life experiences.

Now, with your outline and notes in front of you, write your first complete draft. Don't worry about length at this point. You should be aiming to have much more material than you will eventually use. And don't fret over an opening sentence. The best opening sentences are often written after the rest of the essay has been written. Write until you have used up all of your material. Then, definitely take a break. You should not attempt to revise your draft until the next day, at the earliest. That time away from your writing will help you be more objective when you have to cut material to meet the length requirements.

When you return to your work you will be looking at it with the following criteria in mind:

- Are there particularly strong passages? Mark them to be included.
- Does each point carry much weight? Eliminate those that do not.
- Are certain paragraphs too "busy"? Prune and simplify those that are.
- Are there words and phrases that are unnecessary for meaning and clarity or that are not essential for developing your theme? Is there jargon or words that are meant to show off your facility with the language? Are there cliches? If so, edit or eliminate them. (Reading your essay aloud can help you to spot these.)
- Is the style of writing graceful and succinct? If you have trouble in this regard and have some time, you may want to take a look at Strunk and White's brief classic, *The Elements of Style*, and Joseph Williams's *Style: Toward Clarity and Grace* (see Resources).
- Do your aspirations sound grandiose (e.g., anything that smacks

of "saving the world" through psychology). If so, tone them down but do not eliminate them. Aspirations gain value when they are realistic and achievable.

- Do any of your passages sound as if you're complaining or attacking shortcomings in the field? Rephrase them as positive goals you hope to contribute to, or eliminate them altogether. Complaints turn people off, and your audience may feel that only seasoned psychologists have the perspective needed to make sound judgments of their science and profession.

- Does your last sentence give the reader a sense of completion? Try not to leave readers hanging. Give them a zingy or meaningful sentence that rounds off the discussion.

Finally, it is time to look at the first sentence of your essay. First sentences have a way of influencing the reaction of the reader to the entire essay. Therefore, professional writers spend an incredible amount of time creating, revising, and polishing their leads. You don't have an incredible amount of time, but you should spend enough time to get a first sentence that you can be proud of. Avoid obvious openers, such as "I've always wanted to _____ , and that's why psychology is the field for me." Aim for something professional but attention getting. You might want to take a break and peruse the leads you see in newspaper editorials and feature articles in serious magazines. This can stimulate your own thoughts and provide models that you can play around with in your own essay.

Obtaining Feedback

Your next step in the revision process is to ask one (or preferably more) respected person to read your essays and give you feedback. As with requesting letters of recommendation, it's best to let your reader know how many essays you need comments on, even if you only have one completed when you make your request.

Peter Elbow (1981) has suggested the following questions as springboards for feedback:

What is the quality of the content of the writing: the ideas, the perceptions, the point of view?

How well is the writing organized?

How effective is the language?

Are there mistakes or inappropriate choices in usage [i.e., grammar, spelling, punctuation]?

What was happening to you, moment by moment, as you were reading the piece of writing? (p. 240)

We would add to this list the instruction that your reader put him- or herself in the position of an overworked psychology faculty member who is reading dozens of essays by similarly qualified candidates.

Revising Again

When you get your feedback, take it seriously, particularly those ideas that you know are probably right but wish they weren't because it will require more work on your part. Try to remember that the extra single hour you put in now may mean the difference between getting in or getting rejected by a particular program. When you are finally satisfied with your essay, make sure you follow the program's instructions. If they give you a sheet to type the essay on, use it or create your own sheet that looks exactly like it using your word processor. Do *not* handwrite essays unless explicitly told to do so. As a final step, proofread your essay carefully and then ask someone else to proofread it, too. You don't want a carefully wrought essay marred by a distracting typographical error.

This may seem like a lot of work, particularly when you have 10 essays to do. But each time you go through the cycle it becomes quicker and easier. Some paragraphs can be used in several different essays. And you may even find that some essays seem to come out "whole," obliterating the necessity of some of the steps we've outlined. Remember, your essays do not need to be perfect. The point is to produce solid essays that leave an overall positive impression with your readers and increase your chances for acceptance.

Step 6.5: Fill Out Financial Aid Forms

Many applicants make the mistake of waiting until they are admitted to a program before trying to apply for financial aid. This is a major mistake because the deadline for many financial aid applications is *before* the deadline for applying to many graduate programs (e.g., one university's financial aid applications may be due on January 1, whereas their graduate application forms may not be due until February 15). If you miss such deadlines, loans may be the only resource available to you. This is why we suggested in chapter 5 that you make note of all financial aid deadlines and complete the appropriate forms before (or concurrent with) your graduate school applications. If the deadlines for your programs' financial aid forms are later than the application deadlines, you should first complete your application forms (see step 6.6).

Before you begin filling out forms, make sure you have photocopies of each. You will use these copies to write in your information in pencil. Later, you will type the data or write it legibly in ink on the originals. Many forms will require information from your current or previous year's federal tax forms, so you will save time later by obtaining a copy of these now.

Financial aid forms and their accompanying instructions are typically long and bureaucratic, but it is crucial that you read and heed every instruction and fill in every line. Directors of financial aid have told us that next to missing initial deadlines, the most common mistake graduate school applicants make is *failing to carefully read the information they are sent.* Because these fact sheets and forms are as tedious and boring to read as income tax forms, the tendency is to scan rather than read the material. Don't give in to this temptation! Highlight or star special instructions on your copies. As you carefully read the material, verify the deadlines for each and every form. If you have not yet recorded these deadlines on each financial aid folder, do so now.

Next, order your folders according to application deadlines. Beginning with a copy of the first set of forms, fill in all of the information you have on hand, and make a list of any information that you will need to obtain. Do not procrastinate getting this information, unpleasant though the task may be. Deadlines are for *completed* applications; if you omit a single piece of information, you jeopardize your chances of receiving aid. Once you have completed one or two sets of financial aid forms, the process will go much more quickly and smoothly because you can simply transfer information you already have from one form to another. When you have completed your drafts, carefully type or legibly write in ink the data on all of the forms.

Because this step is typically the most tedious of all of the application steps, it helps to think about the hours you are spending as "paid labor" that may be at a considerably higher rate of pay than many prestigious jobs. For example, if you spend 10 hours on a particular group of forms and receive $1,000 in aid as a result, you have been working at a pay rate of $100 per hour. Even with this incentive, anticipate that you will feel bogged down at times. Try to think of the task as a challenge to your efficiency and build in rewards for yourself for each block of time spent working on your financial aid applications.

Step 6.6: Fill Out Graduate School Application Forms

This is a rather straightforward step, so our instructions will be brief. The three most important things that pertain to filling out your application forms are neatness, accuracy, and completeness. If at all possible, type your responses on the application form. If you must write, print neatly and legibly in black pen. Accuracy includes ensuring both the factual and technical correctness of the information you are providing. Only you can ensure that the facts are correct (your resume and financial aid forms will be handy guides to statistical information such as dates and addresses), but you should have someone else proofread your completed forms for typographical errors as well. You will be dealing with more than a few application forms, so take special care that you do not mix up the sets of materials that you are preparing for each one. Replace each form in its appropriate folder as soon as you are finished working with it.

Step 6.7: Prepare Applications for Mailing

Make sure your application is complete before putting it in the mailing envelope. This means making sure that you have filled out each form entirely, that you have enclosed everything that has been requested, and that you have followed instructions to the letter. Program staff will check to see that each element of the application is present before the application is passed along to the admissions committee for consideration. Incomplete applications may languish in a busy office before you learn that anything is missing. So be sure that your applications are complete before mailing them.

Double-check the addresses to which application and financial aid materials are to be sent. Send program application materials to the address listed on or with these materials, because the address you originally recorded from *Grad Study* may not be the address to which programs want applications sent. Addresses for various financial aid forms are contained in the packets of materials received from the program and the financial aid office.

We recommend including in each application packet a self-addressed, stamped postcard on which you ask the selection committee to confirm receipt of your application. The front of the card should have your address and postage; the back of your card should say something to the effect of "This card acknowledges that _____ (insert name of the university and program) has received a completed application packet."

(Note that a return postcard and a resume should be the only two items that you include that are not specifically requested.) Photocopy each entire application packet before mailing.

The most important thing about mailing applications is to do it in sufficient time to meet the specified deadline (use express mail if there is any doubt). A late application could very well hurt your chances for admission. Record mailing dates on your checklists and follow up at the appropriate time.

Step 6.8: Follow Up

We have suggested this repeatedly throughout this chapter, but it bears saying again: Take responsibility for ensuring that all of your materials are received in time. How can you do that? Here are some general guidelines.

For transcripts and score reports, we have suggested allowing a maximum of six weeks from request to receipt. Most programs will send you acknowledgment of receipt. If you have received no confirmation six weeks after ordering transcripts and score reports, call the program and ask if these materials have been received. Unless the program instructs you otherwise, continue to follow up weekly until you have confirmation of receipt.

For letters of recommendation, you should have included a confirmation postcard to be returned to you by the program on receipt of your recommendations. Allow at least two weeks from the deadline, and if you receive no confirmation by then, call the program. The recommended procedure for following up on receipt of application forms themselves is similar. Usually, you will receive confirmation of receipt through a program's own acknowledgment postcard or through the postcard you supplied with your application. If you have received neither after two weeks from the date you mailed your application, it would be appropriate to call the program to follow up.

We do not recommend making repeated, unnecessary calls to programs. But it is entirely appropriate for you to make a few brief, judicious calls if you have not received information within a reasonable amount of time. Most programs will realize that you are simply assuming proper responsibility for your application.

Conclusion

Now is certainly a time to rejoice. You do not need to wait to hear results before you celebrate the victory you have already achieved. You have negotiated letters of recommendation, even though you may have felt somewhat awkward and uncomfortable asking. You have surmounted the obstacle of anxiety, particularly with regard to writing your essays. You have suffered through the tedium of filling out application forms. In short, you have tended unfailingly, unflinchingly toward your goal of working through the steps in this chapter. Congratulations!

After You've Applied

When we have done our best, we should wait the result in peace.
—*J. Lubbock*

The sense of time passing, as you no doubt know, is highly subjective. When you're busy and under deadline pressures, time flies. You probably experienced this when you were writing your essays and filling out program application forms. When you're passively waiting for something to happen (like the arrival of good news in the mail!), time seems to drag. If you have started to experience this, take heart. There are still some things left to do. Becoming active again will take your mind off the mailbox and increase your sense of mastery and control.

You will have a month or two, if not more, before you hear from programs to which you have applied. Most decisions for fall enrollment are made between March 1 and April 1. Your application materials or confirmation letters should have told you the decision date for particular programs. If not, it is appropriate to call and ask. (Resist the temptation to call for any reason other than this and to confirm receipt of your materials.) In the time you have remaining, we suggest you do three things: (a) Prepare yourself for possible rejection, (b) get ready for any interviews you might be invited to attend, and (c) learn how to accept and reject offers appropriately.

What If You're Rejected?

Throughout this book, we have encouraged you to be realistic but hopeful, and we certainly don't want to dash your hopes now. But the reality is that because available openings are limited, there are thousands of students who would have made excellent psychologists will not get into graduate school in psychology. We suggest that you anticipate that possibility now. If it doesn't occur, then you haven't lost anything. If it does, you will have a strategy in place to deal with it.

We start with the worst-case scenario, one that you may have already played out in your mind: You are rejected at every school to which you've applied. If you can come to terms with this possibility, you are more likely to await the actual result in peace. And, if the worst happens, you will not be overwhelmed; you will be disappointed but not devastated.

Recent advances in psychology have shown that by modifying your cognitions you may be able to cope more effectively with life's downside. For example, Albert Ellis (Ellis & Vega, 1990), Aaron Beck (1988), and David Burns (1990) have shown how challenging and changing the way we talk to ourselves can have a tremendous effect on our resiliency to stress. Psychologist Martin Seligman, who pioneered studies of learned helplessness and depression, has recently shown how optimism can also be learned and used to improve our coping *before* a difficult event occurs (Seligman, 1991). It is Seligman's work on learned optimism that we will focus on in this chapter. By using his ideas, you can "innoculate" yourself against the stress of possibly being rejected.

Seligman (1991) starts with the premise that it is not adverse events per se, such as not getting into graduate school, that result in depression.[1] Rather, it is how you explain those events to yourself (i.e., with an optimistic or pessimistic explanatory style) that determines whether you feel helpless and hence become depressed. Most important for our purposes here, Seligman has shown that "learning beforehand that responding matters prevents learned helplessness" (p. 28) and provides an immunization against depression. Therefore, modifying your anticipatory responses now in a way that fosters optimism may prevent you from being overwhelmed if your worst-case scenario comes true. And you can adapt these strategies for less difficult but still disappointing scenarios, such as being accepted but not getting into your first-choice schools.

Optimistic and pessimistic explanatory styles differ in three ways, according to Seligman (1991), and he identifies pessimism by the presence of 3 Ps: permanency, personalization, and pervasiveness. Optimists see adverse events as temporary setbacks, with short-term repercussions. Pessimists see adverse events as a permanent state and believe that the negative effects will never end. Optimists focus on temporary and specific

---

1. Ellis, Beck, Burns and other cognitive–behavioral therapists also start from this premise. Seligman credits them for some of his ideas about how to learn optimism.

causes for an event, particularly external causes. Pessimists personalize the event, believing their own enduring traits to be the cause. Optimists do not generalize the cause to other events. Pessimists believe that the cause will have pervasive consequences and will project failure onto anticipated future events.

Applying these ideas, let's look at how a pessimistic response to not getting into graduate school might sound: "I'm just not smart enough to be a psychologist. I lack the innate intelligence and talent, and my credentials show it. I feel terrible, and deep down, no matter what else I do, I will always feel second-best. On top of that, everyone else will know I've failed. What's the point in trying again? No reputable program will ever accept me."

Contrast this with an optimistic explanation for the same event: "I'm really disappointed I didn't get in anywhere. I know I'll feel better after a while, especially once I get a perspective and figure out what might have gone wrong. It helps to remember that several thousands of other applicants got rejected as well. Looking at my credentials, I think my GRE scores and lack of research experience may have put me out of the running. Perhaps if I use the next year to prepare more for the GREs and to get some research experience, I can be competitive next year. Just because I was rejected *this* year at *these* schools doesn't mean I'll never be accepted to graduate school in psychology. Besides, there are other alternatives. When I feel better, I will explore my options. Right now I'm going for a swim."

Few people are as pessimistic as the first response indicates or as optimistic as the second, but most will recognize some of their own likely responses as pessimistic. The critical skill is to learn how to dispute them. Take a moment to imagine that you have been rejected by all of your programs and that you are in your most pessimistic frame of mind. Personalize the event and list things you might say that would indicate that you believe the causes and effects to be global and permanent. Write these down sentence by sentence on the right half of a sheet of paper, as we have done in Exhibit 7.1.

Looking at the judgments you may have made, ask yourself whether you would say the same things to a friend. In fact, it may be useful to switch roles at this point. Imagine that a good friend of yours has written those statements and that you want to help her or him counter them with more realistic and useful responses. In helping your friend dispute his or her pessimism, focus on causes that are specific and changeable, relying on evidence rather than on assumptions. Interpret the event as circum-

---

Exhibit 7.1

Pessimistic Responses to Rejection

Pessimistic Thoughts

I'm not grad school material.

I'm not smart enough.

I didn't want it enough.

I feel so incompetent. I'm devastated.

My grades are set in concrete.
Nothing can change so there's no
point in trying.

I should never have applied in the
first place.

I've been found out for the fool I
really am. Now everyone will
know I'm a failure.

I'll never find a career I'll be happy
with. This was my big chance and
I blew it.

If I find another career, it will be set-
tling for second best, so I'll never
see myself as truly successful.

I'm sunk. I don't know what else to
do.

---

scribed rather than pervasive in its consequences, both practically and in terms of self-esteem. Instead of seeing things in black and white, see shades of gray and avoid all-or-nothing thinking and catastrophizing. Above all, be compassionate. Write a refutation of his or her thoughts on the left half of your paper, as is shown in Exhibit 7.2.

If you're stuck in coming up with arguments against pessimism, try filling in the blanks in the following statements: "I don't think it's accurate to label myself _____ just because I didn't get in." "It's not helpful to assume that _____ , when there is little concrete evidence this is true." "Just because I didn't get in doesn't mean _____ will happen." "Hold on, maybe I'm overreacting by saying that I feel _____ . Are things really as bad as all that? I have other things going for me, such as _____ ." "It doesn't help to compare myself to _____ and see him as having it all together. Everyone has limitations and disappointments." "I'm not helpless. I still have alternatives such as _____ and _____ ."

The purpose of all of this is not to sugar-coat disappointment but

Exhibit 7.2

Optimistic Rebuttals to Pessimistic Thoughts

Optimistic Rebuttals	Pessimistic Thoughts
Failure can occur even if motivation and ability are present. In any case, I have evidence of my academic ability. Remember that difficult course I got an A in. And the times my professors remarked on my creative ability. The competition must have really been fierce this year.	I'm not grad school material. I'm not smart enough. I didn't want it enough.
Incompetence is a judgment, not a feeling. And I might be overreacting when I say I'm devastated. What I'm really feeling is disappointed and sad, but these feelings are normal and will pass.	I feel so incompetent. I'm devastated.
Admissions committees evaluate qualifications in context. There are several ways I can improve my qualifications if I decide to apply again.	My grades are set in concrete. Nothing can change so there's no point in trying.
People come to regret not trying more than they ever regret failing.[1] I feel proud of taking a risk.	I should never have applied in the first place.
Most people are aware of the tremendous competition applicants face when applying to graduate school in psychology. People who might judge me harshly are not the people whose opinions count.	I've been found out for the fool I really am. Now everyone will know I'm a failure.
People are typically well-suited for several satisfying careers. What makes for success is not a particular credential but finding a good-enough match between my abilities and a career and being able to adapt and view my choices positively. There are always second chances.	I'll never find a career I'll be happy with. This was my big chance and I blew it.
	If I find another career, it will be settling for second best, so I'll never see myself as truly successful.

continued

Exhibit 7.2, continued

Optimistic Rebuttals	Pessimistic Thoughts
This disappointment gives me the opportunity to spend more time getting to know my career goals and investigating training alternatives. There are people who can help me.	I'm sunk. I don't know what else to do.

[1] We acknowledge Klein and Gotti for this insight in their book *Overcoming Regret: Lessons From the Road Not Taken*, 1992, New York: Bantam Books.

---

to prevent being overcome by temporary defeat. As we mentioned earlier, we don't want to dampen your hope of acceptance. But by reframing your reactions to your worst-case scenario, you will avoid being emotionally paralyzed if it does occur. Later in this chapter, we discuss some concrete alternatives to consider if you are not accepted. But first, let's look at what you might need to do if you are selected as a finalist in one or more programs.

Preselection Interviews

Applying to graduate school in psychology is more like a marathon race than a 5K run. It requires pacing, endurance, and commitment to a long-term goal. Now, as you go into the final stretch, you may feel you don't have any more to give. Fortunately, when you get a letter or a call requesting an interview, your adrenaline will start flowing again: You are at the front of the pack.

Not all programs require preselection interviews, but many do. Those that do typically invite more applicants than will be accepted (how many more varies from program to program). If you are invited, our first piece of advice is, even if you have to borrow the money, go! Our reasoning is this: If a program can select only some of the applicants they interview and they are impressed with the applicants who do show up, you may still be in the running (e.g., by doing well in a telephone interview), but you may be at a disadvantage, particularly in competitive programs with many highly qualified applicants. If you absolutely can't attend, check to see whether the program will consider telephone interviews. But be sure to make it clear to the faculty member you speak with that your inability to attend in person is no reflection on your interest in the program.

As with other steps in the application process, you must prepare thoroughly for this one. No matter how well you have run the race so far, you still have to cross the finish line. This preparation involves five steps. If you have conscientiously worked through the earlier chapters in this book, the first two steps will be a review of what you've already learned.

Step 7.1

Review your research about the program and its faculty. This involves reviewing your program worksheets and any program materials that you were sent. If you did not have the time to thoroughly research programs, learn as much as you can in the time remaining before your interview. Start with the basics—the training model of the program, its areas of emphases, and faculty interests. (You may want to review chapter 5 now and complete relevant steps.)

Step 7.2

Review your qualifications, interests, and goals. Make note of those that make you a particularly good match with the program. Again, many of you have done much of this work earlier and will only need to review your applicant and program worksheets and your notes for your essay. If you didn't have the time to do so earlier, begin to assess yourself from the point of view of the program and what you might contribute to it. When you rehearse answers to potential questions in the next step, you will see whether there is any further work you need to do in this regard.

Step 7.3

Anticipate questions, formulate answers, and rehearse. In Exhibit 7.3, we have listed the kinds of questions applicants are frequently asked. Don't panic when you see how long the list is. You will only be asked a handful of such questions. The more answers you rehearse, however, the more confident you will be.

When you look at each question, jot down a few associations you have to each. You don't need to write full sentences; you just need cue words that will help you articulate answers. Highlight any questions about which you draw a blank or feel that your responses are inadequate. Spend some extra time brainstorming answers to those (you might want to use the cluster technique introduced in chapter 6).

Exhibit 7.3

Interview Questions You May Be Asked

- What are your long-range career goals? Where do you hope to be in five years? In ten?
- What made you decide to pursue a graduate degree in psychology?
- How interested are you in this program?
- What training model are you most interested in? Why?
- Why did you apply to this particular program? Where did you hear about us?
- Why should we accept you into our program?
- How would you describe yourself?
- What are the most important rewards you expect in your graduate training? In your career?
- What are your greatest strengths and weaknesses?
- What two or three accomplishments in your life have given you the most satisfaction?
- How do you work under pressure? How do you handle stress?
- How likely are you to finish your degree? Why do you think you can?
- You will be required to take some rigorous courses that may not be of much interest to you. How do you feel about taking such courses?
- What major academic problem have you faced and how did you deal with it?
- What did you particularly like about your undergraduate education? What did you like least?
- What could you add to our department?
- Have you been involved in any research? If so, was your experience a positive one?
- Give me some examples of your doing more than was required in a course.
- What would you do if (several situations that might occur in graduate school)? For example, if you committed to work with a professor on some research and after two weeks found it impossible to continue, how would you handle that? Or, suppose you had already earned your master's degree and were in a practicum. If someone offered you a great deal of money to work for them full-time, would you delay pursuing your doctorate to do so?
- Is there anything additional we should know about you?
- If you don't mind telling us, what other schools have you applied to?
- Do you have any ambitions to teach?
- How do you feel about giving up a paying job for several years?
- Tell us something interesting about yourself.
- Give us some examples of your creativity, initiative, maturity, and breadth of interest.

Of course, some questions cannot be anticipated. When faced with an unexpected or unusual question, do not panic. Take a few moments to compose a response, keep your answers succinct, and use your academic and career goals as the primary context for your answers. One of the reasons for asking such questions is to see how you react and how well you can express yourself extemporaneously. Whenever possible in these open-ended questions, avoid general and hackneyed answers (such as "I want to help people"), convey your strengths, and emphasize the degree of match between you and the program.

Finally, don't try to answer a question to which you have no answer. Acknowledging the importance of the question and stating that you would have to think about it some more before you could answer is adequate. As in much of life, honesty is still the best policy.

Once you are familiar with the questions and your answers, arrange for someone to role-play an interview with you. Ask them to mark those questions where you stumble. If you don't rehearse with someone else, at the very least practice saying your answers out loud to yourself. It's not enough that you know the answers. You must be able to articulate them.

Step. 7.4

Formulate questions to ask faculty. It is the kiss of death if an applicant comes to an interview without any questions. Again, you need not have many, but if you have none, you may be perceived as passive, dull, or not interested enough in the program. You might start by reviewing your program worksheet and the list of faculty interests that the program may have sent you or you may have researched. There may be questions that your research didn't answer that would be appropriate to ask in an interview. Exhibit 7.4 lists some kinds of questions that are also appropriate to ask. Keep in mind that if you are in a series of one-on-one interviews (see next step), it is perfectly alright to ask some of the same questions in each interview. There are only so many questions you will be able to think of to ask, and for many questions, it's good to get more than one perspective. In case you meet with graduate students during the course of your interview, you may also want to think of questions to ask them. Questions about the atmosphere for students, the supportiveness of faculty, and other questions only students may be able to answer could very well influence your final decision about accepting an offer if it is tendered.

Step 7.5

Find out about the format of the interview. The program may or may not volunteer information about the format of the interview when you are invited to attend. If they don't, it's perfectly okay to ask. Interview formats typically fall into three categories: (a) a sequence of one-on-one

---

Exhibit 7.4

Examples of Questions You Might Ask

- How is the training in this program organized? What is a typical program of study?
- What training model is emphasized? (Ask only if this has not been made explicit in the program materials or through your research.)
- What kind of practicum opportunities would I have? When could these begin?
- Are there opportunities to work with specific populations, such as _____.
- What's the typical success rate for finding jobs for individuals in this program (especially in the specific types of jobs you are interested in)?
- Would I be likely to get financial aid in my first year? If I can't get financial aid in the first year, is there a better possibility in the second or later years?
- What kinds of teaching and research assistantships or traineeships are available? What proportion of first-year students receive them?
- What is the retention rate in this particular program? How long does it typically take to get through?
- I've read about your (or X and Y's) research on _____. What are the possibilities that graduate students could get involved in that research?
- I understand that I will get a master's degree on my way to the PhD. What are the master's and doctoral requirements?
- When are comprehensive exams typically taken?
- Are faculty supportive with regard to original ideas for research?
- Is it possible to talk to a few graduate students in this program?

---

interviews (e.g., you might interview with two or three faculty members separately in the course of one day), (b) group faculty interviews (e.g., you may meet with two or three faculty at one time), and (c) group faculty–group student or panel interviews (e.g., several applicants may meet in a group with several faculty members). You will not get to choose a format, but it does help to know ahead of time just what kind of interview you will be facing.

Preparing for each of these formats is similar (i.e., practicing answering and asking questions). However, the panel interview will require more assertiveness skills on your part. You can't afford to be passive— there will be times in the interview where you will have to claim the floor so that you can communicate your strengths to the faculty. But you can't be too greedy—you should not *always* be the first to speak and you should not insist on far more than your share of air time in comparison with the other candidates. Appropriate assertiveness will stand you in the best stead.

Here are some additional pointers you should keep in mind about interviewing. A certain amount of nervousness is to be expected: You wouldn't be normal if you weren't nervous. The more prepared you are, the less anxious you are likely to be at the time of the interview. Students sometimes avoid rehearsing because it makes them feel anxious, but it is better to be anxious now than to be ill-prepared and to panic the day of the interview. When you go to the interview, bring your folder with your program worksheet, applicant worksheet, and questions to ask, in case you falter and need to jog your memory.

Once at the interview site, be sure to present yourself in a professional manner. Dress appropriately (e.g., business attire), be on time, refrain from smoking or chewing gum, and look directly at the interviewer when speaking or listening. Make sure you understand the questions you are asked. Pause before answering to give yourself time to compose a response that is succinct but thoughtful. Do not try to orchestrate the interview yourself, but follow the interviewer's cues. For example, allow the interviewer to be the one to initiate small talk or a handshake or to invite you to sit down. Wait for the interviewer to ask you if you have any special questions, and if he or she has not done so by the end of the interview, broach the topic politely by asking, "I wonder if you would allow me a few moments to ask you a few questions about the program?" Finally, keep in mind that the faculty are not adversaries and will not expect a star performance. They simply want to get to know you, and they want you, in turn, to learn about their program.

Accepting and Declining Offers

Beginning as early as mid-March, you will receive any of three kinds of notice: acceptance, alternate status, and rejection. As a courtesy to programs and to applicants who may be next in line for offers you decline, you are encouraged to notify programs as soon as possible of your decision to accept or decline an offer. Toward that end, we recommend the following procedure:

- As soon as you have two offers in hand, choose the one that you prefer (you do not have to formally accept just yet unless it is actually your first choice) and decline the other offer.
- As you receive each new offer, repeat this procedure. That is, hold the preferred choice in reserve, and formally decline the less attractive offer.
- As soon as you receive the offer that you want most, accept it and

notify immediately any programs from which offers are pending that you are no longer considering their programs.

Do not hold in reserve more than one offer at a time, because, in effect, you are preventing someone else from being accepted into the program you eventually reject. Other applicants may be compelled to accept offers from programs that are not their first choices; likewise, programs may be losing their first-choice applicants. If every applicant exercises this consideration, everyone's chances of getting their first choices increase.

The proper procedure for accepting or declining offers is to call first, because programs appreciate having either response as soon as possible so that they can proceed to fill remaining openings. Always follow up your call with a brief and polite letter. When declining offers, have the courtesy to thank the program for taking the time to consider you.

If you are given notice of alternate status, it means that your name appears on a rank-ordered list of applicants to whom firm offers will be tendered should other applicants decline offers and openings become available. Alternate status does not reflect poorly on your desirability as an applicant; you would not be selected as an alternate if you were not well-qualified. As with firm offers, try to make a decision quickly in order to give other alternate candidates a chance. If you do not yet have to make a decision about another offer and you are interested in the program you are an alternate for, notify the program that you wish to remain on the list. At any time that you are certain you do not wish to consider the alternate program further, decline officially and immediately.

Being an alternate can be problematic. What do you do, for example, if you are an alternate for your first- or second-choice program but have a firm offer from a less desired program? Each program is anxious for your decision, but you are reluctant to accept the firm offer in case an opening becomes available for you in your preferred program. In a situation such as this, it would be appropriate and acceptable for you to contact the program for which you are an alternate, explain the situation, and ask whether they can tell you where you are on the list. Most programs will be willing to tell you what they can in this situation. Knowing how far up or down you are on the list may help you decide whether you should wait a little longer or accept another offer. You may get to a point where you will have to forego an alternate offer from your preferred program and accept a firm offer from a less-preferred program if you want to ensure your enrollment.

Your ability and willingness to readily decide on offers you receive may well be contingent on financial aid offers. A common scenario is as follows. You have two offers in hand. One is from your first-choice program, but you have not yet received notice of financial support to attend that program. The other is from a less-preferred program, but it is accompanied by a generous financial aid offer. Do you go ahead and accept the offer from your favored program and risk not receiving financial aid? Or do you settle for the program that you are certain you can afford? Applicants may frequently find themselves compelled to make premature decisions when acceptance and financial aid offers are not made simultaneously. It is important for you to know that in most cases, you have the option of delaying your decision until April 15, if circumstances require you to.

The April 15th option is the result of a resolution adopted by the Council of Graduate Departments of Psychology in 1965 and modified in 1981 and 1988. Graduate programs must sign an agreement that they will abide by this resolution in order to be listed in *Grad Study*. The resolution and its modifications appear in the front of *Grad Study* under "Rules for Acceptance of Offers for Admission and Financial Aid." Essentially, programs agree not to require applicants to make a decision prior to April 15. This time allowance enables applicants to withhold their decision without forfeiting the offer if they should need to wait for a financial aid offer that is crucial to their decision. The resolution also makes it possible for applicants to reject an offer they have already accepted if they do so prior to April 15, but only if they obtain a written release from the program to which they were formerly accepted. Finally, the resolution strongly discourages applicants from soliciting or accepting any other offers after April 15. The resolution helps to protect applicants from being pressured to make premature decisions, and it protects programs against a plethora of withdrawals subsequent to acceptance.

Is it possible for you to change your mind after you have accepted an offer? The preceding discussion of the April 15 resolution should answer your question. We strongly discourage withdrawing acceptance, but we realize that it is necessary from time to time. As was stipulated in the preceding discussion, you may withdraw your acceptance of admission or financial aid, as long as you do so before April 15 and submit your resignation in writing. The program you are opting for instead will require you to have a written release from the program that previously accepted you.

One final note: When you have made your decision, call or write your recommenders to thank them again and let them know where you were accepted and where you have decided to go. Faculty truly care about the outcome, and they appreciate the feedback that their hard work on letters of recommendation may have helped.

Alternatives If You Are Not Accepted

Being rejected by every program you applied to is certainly disappointing, as we discussed earlier, but it does not *necessarily* mean you should give up your ambitions to be a psychologist or to pursue a career in a related field. What should you do now? Basically, you have three alternatives (or four, if you initially applied only to doctoral programs and are now considering master's programs): reapply to other graduate psychology programs for the same school year (or apply to master's programs if you were rejected by doctoral programs); reapply to the same or apply to other graduate psychology programs for the following school year; or consider alternatives to a graduate degree in psychology.

To decide which alternative to pursue, you might first ask yourself whether it is possible that you set your sights too high and applied to too many programs that had very high admission standards. Perhaps programs you calculated as strong bets were actually long shots. You can test this theory by systematically reassessing your qualifications against admission requirements. If, in fact, your credentials were very good, it is possible that the competition for this year or for the programs you chose was exceptionally intense, that is, that you were up against an unusual abundance of well-qualified applicants. Sometimes the rejection letters you receive from programs will give you some clues to the reasons for your rejection, and, depending on whether your weaknesses can be addressed, you might feel encouraged to try those or other programs again. It is a good idea to talk with a respected professor of psychology and have them help you with your reassessment. Those who wrote your letters of recommendation will want to know what happened, and they may be able to help you decide what to do next. Let's now consider some alternatives.

Reapplying for the Same School Year

If you were chosen as an alternate by any program, there is still a possibility of receiving a firm offer. It is not unheard of to receive an offer only a few weeks before the beginning of the semester. So one option you have is to remain on alternate lists and keep in contact with the program periodically to find out if you are moving up the list.

If you were not an alternate but you believe in your qualifications and are determined to gain enrollment for the coming fall, you can try sending out another round of applications to a new set of programs. There are several ways to identify possibilities. One is to take another look at programs you classified as being strong bets, when you did your program research, but did not send applications to. Remember, strong bets are programs for which your grades, scores, and coursework exceed requirements. Contact those programs and find out whether they will still accept applications; if they have not filled all of their openings, they may welcome an application from you. Another strategy is to reexamine programs that were on your preliminary list but did not make your final list. If any of these programs now appeal to you and your qualifications exceed their requirements, call and find out whether they will still accept applications. You could also initiate new research to identify programs that have very late application deadlines, that accept applications for entry in semesters other than fall, or that are in lesser demand (e.g., perhaps because of their accreditation status or geographic location) and are, therefore, more likely to have unfilled openings. Finally, the APA Education Directorate compiles a list each spring of programs that have openings after April 15. The list is released in early June. To receive the list between April 15 and June 30, *write* to Graduate Openings, c/o American Psychological Association, Education Directorate, at the address listed in the Resources. If your reapplication attempts fail, you may want to consider waiting another year to apply.

Reapplying for the Following School Year

If you decide to wait it out a year and try again, there are basically two things you should do in the interval: reselect programs and enhance your qualifications. In deciding which programs to apply to, first determine whether to reapply to any of the same programs. Programs for which you were chosen as an alternate but never gained a slot are attractive possibilities because these programs were obviously interested in you. For programs that rejected you firmly, we recommend that you contact them before attempting a reapplication and that you ask whether they would be willing to consider another application from you. If they say no, you have little choice but to cross these programs off your list. You will also want to apply to some new programs, in which case you will have to do your program research again, but because you are experienced now, this will take you much less time. This time you may want to set your sights a little lower and seek out programs whose admission requirements are less stringent. Be sure to take another look at programs that interested you particularly in the beginning of your initial research but that you ended up not applying to.

To increase your chances of acceptance the second time around, you should use the time available to work on your credentials. This could include taking or retaking courses, retaking tests, or obtaining some solid research or clinical experience. You may want to review chapter 4 for advice on enhancing your qualifications, to determine what kind of improvements would benefit you the most. If a program has indicated that they will consider another application from you, you might tell them that you wish to enhance your credentials before reapplying, and tactfully ask whether they have any specific recommendations (they may actually recommend that you earn a master's degree first; we discuss this next). Any time you spend on improvement will be time well spent: If you are able to strengthen your credentials, it will be viewed positively by any program that is reconsidering you, and you will be a better qualified applicant for any other programs you choose.

Finally, do not make the mistake of applying to one type of program and then trying to switch to another (e.g., apply to study developmental psychology and then hope to switch to counseling or clinical psychology). Programs view these tactics very negatively, and many prohibit switching altogether.

Applying to Master's Programs

An option for students who were rejected by doctoral programs is to consider master's programs in psychology. Master's programs often have less stringent qualifications than doctoral programs, so you may have a better chance of competing. You should, however, keep three things firmly in mind. One is that a master's degree may not be an adequate credential for the field in which you're interested (e.g., to be a clinical psychologist requires a doctoral degree; to teach in a university setting requires the same). Second, if your eventual goal is a doctorate, few or none of your master's credits may transfer (this depends on the school and program where you wish to get your doctorate). So, even if you eventually get into a doctoral psychology program, you may in effect be starting all over again. And finally, if what you really want is a doctorate, a master's degree may never satisfy you.

On the other hand, a master's degree in psychology is an excellent credential for many types of jobs. Contact people in the areas of psychology in which you're interested and ask them if they know of job opportunities in that area for master's degree recipients. Network to get names of those working in that area with a master's degree, and call them. Ask about their careers and whether they have been hampered professionally by not having a doctorate; if so, inquire about these limitations. If you are satisfied with the career potential in your field for master's recipients, you may redefine your program requirements and preferences and begin the kind of research into programs you completed in chapter 5.

If you decide to obtain your master's degree but eventually wish to pursue a doctorate in psychology, start now to pave your way. Research doctoral programs that interest you to find out whether they accept credits from a terminal master's program and, if so, which ones. Then look for master's programs that offer those courses. While you're earning your master's degree, get the most out of the program that you can by becoming involved in research, by writing articles for professional meetings at which student papers are presented, and perhaps by becoming a junior author on an article submitted for publication. Strive to know your professors well and to become well known to them, so that they will be amply qualified to write letters of recommendation for doctoral programs. Finally, endeavor to get high grades (remember, a "C" in graduate school is often considered failing).

Alternatives to Psychology

A reassessment of your options and qualifications may suggest that your chances of being accepted into a graduate psychology program would probably not improve significantly, even with an additional year of preparation. If this is the case, you need not feel that you have wasted your time by majoring in psychology or taking requisite courses, nor should you abandon hope that your interests in psychology can be satisfied through some other profession. Because psychological knowledge can be applied in virtually any occupational arena, you will still be able to make good use of your academic preparation. Indeed, many psychology undergraduates have gone on to achieve remarkable success as entrepreneurs, writers, teachers, lawyers, business executives, marketing specialists, artists, and so on—in short, they wear a surprising variety of hats. Psychology, the science of mind and behavior, provides a strong foundation for understanding and interpreting the world and the people in it.

If you are still interested in pursuing a profession directly related to psychology, there may be other graduate degrees that will get you where you want to go and perhaps even in a shorter time. For example, applicants interested in clinical psychology might look into social work programs with a specialization in mental health or clinical social work. Although such programs do not qualify you to perform psychological testing (only an advanced degree in psychology can do that), many of them do provide a solid foundation in individual, couples, family, and group psychotherapy. After a required number of supervised hours of clinical work and after passing a written and/or oral examination, social workers can be licensed to practice clinical social work independently (e.g., in private practice). Individuals interested in community or health psychology can also find social work programs with community and health specializations. Many education departments also offer a degree in counseling or in marriage and family therapy. In considering the alternatives to clinical psychology, make sure you learn exactly what is required in terms of coursework, supervision, and practica to earn a license in the states in which you might wish to practice.

People with interests that intersect with fields other than psychology might want to look into programs in those fields. For example, someone with an interest in organizational psychology might look into graduate programs housed in business schools that emphasize organizational development. Someone interested in research involving group behavior might look into a graduate degree in sociology. Others who are interested in language and psychology might look into graduate linguistics programs. Likewise, those interested in psychobiology might consider a graduate degree in biology.

In making these decisions, don't feel you have to go it alone. Talk to people informally, make appointments with people who have the alternate degree you're thinking of acquiring, and, if you're stuck, contact your school's career counseling center or consult with a reputable career planning specialist. The bottom line is to care enough about yourself and your future to reassess what it is that you want to do from day to day, in what kind of setting, with whom, and for what purpose. It could well be that you can find equally good training for the career you have outlined for yourself in a field related to psychology.

Conclusion

In this chapter, you have completed the application cycle. From your first glimpse into *Grad Study* to your interview on campus, we hope that this book has been helpful to you. For those of you who have been admitted, congratulations. We wish you the best as you enter the community of psychology scholars.

Thinking of the majority of you who were not admitted, this has been a difficult chapter to write. The idea that many of you who worked hard on your applications and who have the potential to become competent psychologists will not be admitted largely because of the limited number of training slots is disheartening. On the other hand, with any luck, those same qualities that may have made you an excellent psychologist will serve you well in whichever other path you choose. Psychology is only one house in the community of vocations. And, as André Gide has been quoted as saying, "It is a rule of life that when one door closes, another door always opens."

References

Allen, W. (1986). *The fire in the birdbath and other disturbances*. New York: Norton.

Alletzhauser, H. L., & McConnell, S. C. (1993). *The Doctor of Psychology degree: A guide for prospective students*. Unpublished manuscript, School of Professional Psychology, Wright State University, Dayton, OH.

American Psychological Association. (1986). *Careers in psychology*. Washington, DC: Author.

Barrom, C. P., Shadis, Jr., W. R., & Montgomery, L. M. (1988). PhDs, PsyDs, and real-world constraints on scholarly activity: Another look at the Boulder model. *Professional Psychology: Research and Practice, 19*, 93–101.

Beck, A. T. (1988). *Cognitive therapy and the emotional disorders*. New York: NAL/Dutton.

Benjamin, L. T., Jr. (1986). Why don't they understand us? A history of psychology's public image. *American Psychologist, 41*, 941–946.

Burns, D. (1990). *The feeling good handbook*. New York: NAL/Dutton.

Cesa, I. L., & Fraser, S. C. (1989). A method for encouraging the development of good mentor–protege relationships. *Teaching of Psychology, 16*, 125–128.

Clark, M. J., Hartnett, R. T., & Baird, L. L. (1976). *Assessing dimensions of quality in doctoral education*. Princeton, NJ: Educational Testing Service.

Cone, J. D., & Foster, S. L. (1993). *Dissertations and theses from start to finish: Psychology and related fields*. Washington, DC: American Psychological Association.

Cronan-Hillix, T., Gensheimer, L. K., Cronan-Hillix, W. A., & Davidson, W. S. (1986). Students' views of mentors in psychology graduate training. *Teaching of Psychology, 13*, 123–127.

Eddy, B., Lloyd, P. J., & Lubin, B. (1987). Enhancing the application to doctoral professional programs: Suggestions from a national survey. *Teaching of Psychology, 14*, 160–163.

Elbow, P. (1981). *Writing with power*. New York: Oxford University Press.

Ellis, A., & Vega, G. (1990). *Self-management: Strategies for personal success*. New York: Institute for Rational-Emotive Therapy.

Evans, R. B., Sexton, V. S., & Cadwallader, T. C. (1992). *The American Psychological Association: A historical perspective*. Washington, DC: American Psychological Association.

Freedheim, D. K., Freudenberger, H. J., Kessler, J. W., Messer, S. B., Peterson, D. R., Strupp, H. H., & Wachtel, P. L. (Eds.). (1992). *History of psychotherapy: A century of change*. Washington, DC: American Psychological Association.

Gilbert, L. A., & Rossman, K. M. (1992). Gender and the mentoring process for women:

Implications for professional development. *Professional Psychology: Research and Practice, 23*, 233–238.

Haynes, S. N., Lemsky, C., & Sexton-Radek, K. (1987). Why clinicians infrequently do research. *Professional Psychology: Research and Practice, 18*, 515–519.

Hilgard, E. R. (1987). *Psychology in America: A historical survey.* New York: Harcourt Brace Jovanovich.

Jarrow, J., Baker, B., Hartman, R., Harris, R., Lesh, K., Redden, M., & Smithson, J. (1991). *How to choose a college: Guide for the student with a disability* (3rd ed.). Washington, DC: HEATH Resource Center.

Klein, C., & Gotti, R. (1992). *Overcoming regret: Lessons from the road not taken.* New York: Bantam Books.

Koch, S., & Leary, D. E. (1992). *A century of psychology as science.* Washington, DC: American Psychological Association.

Kohout, J. L., & Wicherski, M. M. (1992). *1991 salaries in psychology.* Washington, DC: American Psychological Association.

Kohout, J. L., & Wicherski, M. M. (1993). *1991 doctorate employment survey.* Washington, DC: American Psychological Association.

McWade, P. (1993). *Financing graduate school.* Princeton, NJ: Peterson's Guides.

Parker, L. E., & Detterman, D. K. (1988). The balance between clinical and research interests among Boulder model graduate students. *Professional Psychology: Research and Practice, 19*, 342–344.

Preamble. (1990, January). National Conference on Scientist–Practitioner Education and Training for the Professional Practice of Psychology, Gainesville, FL.

Rico, G. L. (1983). *Writing the natural way.* Los Angeles, CA: Tarcher.

Seligman, M. P. (1991). *Learned optimism.* New York: Knopf.

Snepp, F. P., & Peterson, D. R. (1988). Evaluative comparison of PsyD and PhD students by clinical internship supervisors. *Professional Psychology: Research and Practice, 19*, 180–183.

Walfish, S., Stenmark, D. E., Shealy, J. S., & Shealy, S. E. (1989). Reasons why applicants select clinical psychology graduate programs. *Professional Psychology: Research and Practice, 20*, 350–354.

Resources

General Resources

The following list of organizations and publications may be useful to all applicants to graduate programs in psychology. Because many of the resources here and under Specialized Resources refer to directorates and offices of the American Psychological Association (APA), the main address and phone number of the APA are listed here; specific directorates and phone numbers are presented when applicable.

Organizations

American Psychological Association (APA)
750 First Street, NE
Washington, DC 20002-4242
(202) 336-5500

APA Division Services
See the APA address listed above
(202) 336-6013

APA Education Directorate
Education in Psychology
See the APA address listed above
(202) 336-5963

American Psychological Association of Graduate Students (APAGS)
750 First Street, NE
Washington, DC 20002-4242
(202) 336-6093

APA Order Department (for books and journals)
P.O. Box 2710
Hyattsville, MD 20784
(202) 336-5510 or 1-800-374-2721
FAX (202) 336-5502

Psi Chi
National Honor Society in Psychology
(4-year colleges, universities, and graduate schools)
407 East Fifth Street, Suite B
Chattanooga, TN 37403
(615) 756-2044

Psi Beta
National Honor Society in Psychology
(2-year colleges)
407 East Fifth Street, Suite B
Chattanooga, TN 37403
(615) 265-6555

Publications

American Psychological Association. (1986). *Careers in psychology*. Washington, DC: Author. (Contact the APA Order Department at address, phone, or fax listed above.)

American Psychological Association. *Graduate study in psychology* (biyearly publication with yearly updates). Washington, DC: Author. (Available at most university libraries, or contact the APA Order Department at address, phone, or fax listed above.)

Lefferts, A., VonVorys-Norton, B., Koether, P., & Williams, P. (Eds.). (1993). *Peterson's guide to graduate and professional programs: An overview* (27th ed.). Princeton, NJ: Peterson's Guides. (Available at local bookstores.)

Peterson's annual guides to graduate study. (1993; 27th ed.). Princeton, NJ: Peterson's Guides. (Available at most university libraries.)

Specialized Resources

The following organizations and publications are aimed at specific populations of applicants, specific areas of psychology, or specific aspects of the application process. Organizations are listed first and publications second.

Areas of Concentration in Psychology

APA Division Services
See APA address in General Resources
(202) 336-6013

(See Appendix B of this book for a description of divisions. Some divisions have information on training and careers in specific areas of psychology (see below); contact Division Services for student representatives and representatives for education and training in a particular division.)

American Psychologist. In July of every year, this journal lists officers, boards, committees, division officers, and other representatives of the APA, as well as regional and state psychological associations, that may be of particular interest to specific applicant populations or those interested in specific areas of psychology. (Available at most university libraries.)

American Psychological Association. (1993). *Journals in psychology*. Washington, DC: Author. Examining these journals can help clarify the areas of concentration in psychology that you might be interested in. (Available at most university libraries, or contact the APA Order Department at address, phone, or fax listed in General Resources.)

Careers and Training in Psychology (Selected)

Neuroscience training programs in North America. (1990; to be updated in 1994).
Society for Neuroscience
11 Dupont Circle, NW
Suite 500
Washington, DC 20036

The following brochures are available from APA divisions. Contact APA Division Services at the address and phone number listed in General Resources.

"Careers in Educational and Psychological Measurement"
Available from Division 5—Evaluation, Measurement, and Statistics.

"Guide to Graduate Programs in Developmental Psychology"
Available from Division 7—Developmental Psychology.

"What is a Personality/Social Psychologist?"
Available from Division 8—Personality and Social Psychology.

"Training in Pediatric Psychology"
Available from Section V—Pediatric Psychology of Division 12—Clinical Psychology.

"Military Psychology: An Overview"
Available from Division 19—Military Psychology.

"A Guide to Doctoral Study in Adult Development and Aging"
Available from Division 20—Adult Development and Aging.

"A Career in Consumer Psychology"
Available from Division 23—Consumer Psychology.

Disability-Related Concerns

APA Committee on Disability Issues in Psychology
Contact the APA Public Interest Directorate at the APA address listed under General Resources, or phone (202) 336-6050.

HEATH Resource Center
American Council on Education
One Dupont Circle, NW
Suite 800
Washington, DC 20036-1193
(202) 939-9320; (800) 544-3284

Financial aid for students with disabilities. (1989).
HEATH Resource Center
(see address above)

How to choose a college: Guide for the student with a disability. (1991; 3rd ed.).
HEATH Resource Center
(see address above)

Information from HEATH
Bimonthly newsletter
(see address above)

Resource directory. (1991–1992).
HEATH Resource Center
(see address above)

Dissertations and Theses

Cone, J. D., & Foster, S. L. (1993). *Dissertations and theses from start to finish: Psychology and related fields*. Washington, DC: American Psychological Association.

Ethnic Minority Concerns—General (see also Ethnic Minority— Financial Aid)

APA Committee on Ethnic Minority Affairs
Contact the APA Public Interest Directorate, Office of Ethnic Minority Affairs (OEMA) at the APA address listed under General Resources, or call (202) 336-6050.

Contact information for the following four associations can be obtained from OEMA at (202) 336-6050.

Asian American Psychological Association
Association of Black Psychologists

National Hispanic Psychological Association
The Society of Indian Psychologists

American Psychological Association. (1993). *Directory of ethnic minority professionals in psychology.* Public Interest Directorate, Office of Ethnic Minority Affairs, address listed under General Resources, or call (202) 336-6047.

Ethnic Minority—Financial Aid

Dorothy Danforth Compton Minority Fellowship Program
(Fellowships are administered through 10 specific universities. For general information, see following address and phone number.)

Danforth Foundation
231 South Bemiston Avenue
St. Louis, MO 63105-1903
(314) 862-6200

Ford Foundation Predoctoral and Dissertation Fellowships for Minorities
The Fellowship Office, National Research Council
2101 Constitution Avenue, NW
Washington, DC 20418
(202) 334-2872

Minority Fellowship Program
American Psychological Association
Address listed under General Resources, or call (202) 336-6027.

Minority Undergraduate Students of Excellence (MUSE)
Public Interest Directorate, Office of Ethnic Minority Affairs
Address listed under General Resources, or call (202) 336-6050.

National Science Foundation Minority Graduate Fellowships
The Fellowship Office, National Research Council
2101 Constitution Avenue, NW
Washington, DC 20418
(202) 334-2872

American Psychological Association. (1992). *Financial aid resources for ethnic minorities pursuing undergraduate, graduate, and post-doctoral study in psychology.* Public Interest Directorate, Office of Ethnic Minority Affairs, address listed under General Resources, or call (202) 336-6050.

Bureau of Indian Affairs Higher Education Grants and Scholarships
Post Secondary Education
1849 C Street, NW
Mail Stop 3512-MIB
Washington, DC 20240
(202) 208-4871

Directory of financial aids for minorities. (1993–1995). Available in university financial aid offices and libraries, or contact Reference Service Press, 1100 Industrial Road, Suite 9, San Carlos, CA 94070; (415) 594-0743.

Financial Aid—General (see also specific populations of applicants)

A selected list of fellowship opportunities and aids to advanced education for U.S. citizens and foreign nationals. (Free)

Publication Office
National Science Foundation
1800 G Street, NW
Washington, DC 20550
(202) 357-7861

Grants register. New York: St. Martin's Press. (Published biannually; available at most university financial aid offices and libraries.)

McWade, P. (1993). *Financing graduate school*. Princeton, NJ: Peterson's Guides. (Available at local bookstores.)

Peterson's grants for graduate study. (1991; 3rd ed.). Princeton, NJ: Peterson's Guides. (Available at most university financial aid offices and libraries.)

Gay and Lesbian Concerns

APA Committee on Lesbian and Gay Concerns
Contact the APA Public Interest Directorate at the address listed under General Resources, or call (202) 336-6050.

APA Division 44—Society for the Psychological Study of Lesbian and Gay Issues. Contact APA Division Services at the address and phone number listed under General Resources.

American Psychological Association Committee on Lesbian and Gay Issues. (1993). *Graduate faculty in psychology interested in lesbian and gay issues*. Contact the APA Public Interest Directorate, Gay and Lesbian Concerns, at the address listed under General Resources, or call (202) 336-6050.

Buhrke, R. A., & Douce, L. A. (1991). Training issues for counseling psychologists in working with lesbian women and gay men. *Counseling Psychologist, 19*, 216–234.

Cantor, J. M. (1991). *Being gay and being a graduate student: Twice the memberships, four times the problems*. Paper presented at the 99th Annual Convention of the American Psychological Association, San Francisco, CA. Available from the American Psychological Association of Graduate Students, 750 First Street, NE, Washington, DC 20002, or call (202) 336-6093.

Cantor, J. M. (1992). *Homophobia in psychology programs: A survey of graduate students*. Paper presented at the 100th Annual Convention of the American Psychological Association, Washington, DC. ERIC Document Reproduction Services, No. ED 351 618.

International Students

College handbook foreign students' supplement. (1994).

College Board Publications
Dept. .S81, Box 886
New York, NY 10101-0886
(212) 713-8165

Graduate study in the United States: A guide for prospective international graduate students. (1991).

Publications
Council of Graduate Schools
One Dupont Circle, NW, Suite 430
Washington, DC 20036-1173
(202) 223-3791

Guide to state residency requirements. (1991).

College Board Publications
Dept. .S81, Box 886
New York, NY 10101-0886
(212) 713-8165

Selected list of fellowship opportunities and aids to advanced education for U.S. citizens and foreign nationals. (Free)

Publication Office
National Science Foundation
1800 G Street, NW
Washington, DC 20550
(202) 357-7861

Test of English as a Foreign Language (TOEFL) Bulletin

ETS Order Services
Mail Stop 21 H
1440 Lower Ferry Road
Trenton, NJ 08618
(609) 771-7243

Standardized Tests

Graduate Record Exam (GRE)
GRE Registration & Information Bulletin (updated yearly)

Graduate Record Examinations
Educational Testing Service
P.O. Box 6000
Princeton, NJ 08541-6000
(For computerized testing on short notice, call the National Registration Center at 1-800-967-1100.)

Katzman, J. (1994). *The Princeton Review: Cracking the GRE*. New York: Random House.

Martison, T. H. (1993). *GRE supercourse* (3rd ed.). Englewood Cliffs, NJ: Prentice Hall.

Potter, M. C., Ney, J. W., & Cross, J. R. (1993). *GRE time saver: An efficient guide to the General Test*. Maple City, MI: Great Lakes Press.

Research and Education Association. (1993). *GRE General Test preparation* (rev. ed.). Piscataway, NJ: Author.

Research and Education Association. (1993). *GRE Psychology Test preparation* (rev. ed.). Piscataway, NJ: Author.

Tarlow, D. M. (1993). *Graduate Record Exam (GRE): Student guide*. St. Louis, MO: Datar.

Miller Analogies Test (MAT)

Bulletin of Information and List of Testing Centers With 60 Practice Items for the MAT. (updated yearly)

The Psychological Corporation
555 Academic Court
San Antonio, TX 78204-2498

Bader, W., Burt, D. S., & Steinberg, E. P. (1991). *MAT: Miller Analogies Test* (4th ed.). Englewood Cliffs, NJ: Prentice Hall.

Rudman, J. (1991). *Miller Analogies Test (MAT)*. Syosset, NY: National Learning Corporation.

Sternberg, R. J. (1989). *Barron's how to prepare for the Miller Analogies Test—MAT* (5th ed.). Hauppauge, NY: Barron's Educational Series.

Time Management and Combatting Procrastination

Burns, D. (1990). A prescription for procrastinators. *The feeling good handbook*. New York: NAL/Dutton.

Fiore, N. (1989). *The NOW Habit: A strategic program for overcoming procrastination and enjoying guilt-free play*. Los Angeles: Tarcher.

Schenkel, S. (1992). *Giving away success: Why women get stuck and what to do about it* (rev. ed.). New York: HarperPerrenial.

Women—Financial Aid (see also Women—General)

American Psychological Association. (1993). *A directory of selected scholarship, fellowship, and other financial aid opportunities for women and ethnic minorities in psychology and related fields*. Contact the Women's Programs Office, Public Interest Directorate, at the address listed under General Resources, or call (202) 336-6044.

Directory of financial aids for women. (1993–1995).
Reference Services Press
1100 Industrial Road, Suite 9
San Carlos, CA 94070
(415) 594-0743

Women—General (see also Women—Financial Aid)

APA Division 35—Psychology of Women. Contact APA Division Services at address under General Resources, or call (202) 336-6013. Division 35 has a Mentoring Program and a Students and New Graduates Committee.

APA Women's Programs, Public Interest Directorate, at the address listed under General Resources, or call (202) 336-6050.

Association for Women in Psychology
1993 Contact: Colleen Gregory, PhD
Membership Chair
41 Abbey Road
Fairfield, CT 06430

American Psychological Association. (1994). *Graduate faculty interested in the psychology of women.* Contact the Women's Programs Office at the address listed under General Resources, or call (202) 336-6050.

Writing

American Psychological Association. (1983). *Publication manual of the American Psychological Association* (3rd ed.). Washington, DC: Author.

Elbow, P. (1981). *Writing with power.* New York: Oxford University Press.

Rico, G. L. (1983). *Writing the natural way.* Los Angeles: Tarcher.

Strunk, W., Jr., & White, E. B. (1979). *The elements of style* (3rd ed.). New York: Macmillan.

Williams, J. M. (1990). *Style: Toward clarity and grace.* Chicago: University of Chicago Press.

Appendix A: Timetable for Early Planners

In chapter 1, we presented a "typical" timetable for students beginning the application process in September of their senior year in college. In this appendix, we offer students beginning to prepare during their junior year in college[1] an earlier plan that allows for additional activities that can considerably enhance your chances of getting into graduate school in psychology. If you are starting this process during the summer before your senior year in college, begin with that section of the early plan and check the previous sections to see if there are things you still have time to become involved in (e.g., perhaps it's still possible to help with some research in the psychology department or to spend a few hours a week volunteering in a human services agency). Not every one of these junior-year tasks will be necessary, but every one that you do may enhance your chances of success.

Junior Year (or before)

_____ Read chapters 2, 3, and 4 of this book.
_____ Start reading about careers in psychology (see chapter 3 and Resources). Explore your interests with faculty.
_____ Attend colloquia and other events sponsored by your psychology department.

---

1. For potential applicants who have been out of school for a while, translate these time frames into months or years (e.g., the junior year would mean beginning approximately two years before you plan to attend; September of the senior year would mean beginning exactly one year before you plan to attend).

_____ Meet with one or more psychology professors to determine the electives in math, science, computer science, psychology, and other areas that might be an asset in applying to graduate school (see chapter 4).

_____ Find out faculty research interests at your school, read their articles, and make acquaintance with those whose work interests you.

_____ Take a class or two with the professors identified above; volunteer to assist them in their research (the latter will give you invaluable experience and is also a way of letting your professors get to know you as a prelude to your asking for a letter or recommendation).

_____ Find out if you are qualified to join Psi Chi and decide whether to become a member.

_____ Consider getting research and other field-related experiences pertinent to those areas of psychology you are interested in (see chapter 4).

_____ Begin to get acquainted with the publication *Graduate Study in Psychology*, which you can find in your library or psychology department. Make note of any programs that appeal to you.

_____ Check out student or career counseling services at your school to see what resources and advising they have with regard to applying to graduate school.

_____ Find out about state, regional, and national psychology conferences. Attend those that interest you if you are able.

_____ Send away for bulletins for the GREs and MAT. Use study guides or attend a course to prepare (see Resources). Take practice exams to estimate what your score may be.

Summer Before Your Senior Year

_____ Read chapter 5 of this book.

_____ Photocopy or modify the worksheet summarizing your qualifications and requirements.

_____ Find out what programs exist by carefully studying *Graduate Study in Psychology* and related catalogs.

_____ Compile a preliminary list of programs that offer the area of concentration, degree, and training model that appeal to you.

_____ Using the worksheets provided in chapter 5, compare your qualifications with admission requirements.

_____ Contact those programs that seem a good match to obtain additional information about the program *and* about financial aid. Ask for an application packet. Study this information carefully.

_____ Using the strategy outlined and worksheets provided in chapter 5, compile a final list of programs that you will apply to. If you can afford it and it seems worthwhile, visit the campuses of programs that interest you most or that raise the most questions for you.

_____ Call the financial aid offices of all of the schools you will be applying to. Ask for an information packet about the aid available to graduate students, as well as any forms you will need to complete to be considered for financial aid. Ask if there is anyone else you should be talking to regarding other potential sources of aid.

_____ Go to the career planning or student center or library at your undergraduate school to research financial aid opportunities in addition to the ones offered by the universities to which you are applying.

_____ Read chapter 6 of this book. Plan and schedule your application strategy. Pay careful attention to application deadlines, particularly with regard to financial aid, which often has *earlier* deadlines than admissions applications.

_____ Record goals for each week that remains before your applications must be submitted.

_____ Calculate application fees and make sure you have enough money to cover them (some schools waive this fee because of financial hardship; this needs to be checked with each individual school).

_____ Begin planning how you will obtain the money for any preselection interviews you may be required to attend.

September of Your Senior Year

_____ Apply in the first week of September (or earlier) to take the GREs in October and to take the next scheduled MAT. (Continue reviewing on a regular basis.)

_____ Submit a request for your undergraduate transcript, which you will include in your packet for those who will write letters of recommendation.

_____ Prepare a resume for the same purpose.

_____ Begin to finalize your decision regarding which professors to ask to write these letters.[2]

_____ Begin thinking about the various essay questions each program requires. Allow time for your ideas to germinate.

October

_____ Take the GREs and the MAT; request that scores be sent to all schools to which you will apply.

_____ Begin contacting individuals from whom you might request letters of recommendation.

_____ Begin filling out your financial aid and application forms.

_____ Write first drafts of essays; ask for feedback from others.

November

_____ Request that your undergraduate transcript(s) be sent to all of the institutions you are applying to. Make sure that your transcripts will be sent by your earliest application deadline.

_____ Finalize financial aid forms.

_____ Finalize application forms.

_____ Get feedback and write the final drafts of essays.

_____ Supply individuals who will write your letters of recommendation with the packet you prepared earlier, including forms sent by each school.

December

_____ Carefully prepare _each_ application for mailing. Be sure to photocopy each in its entirety. Consider registered mail if you can afford it.

---

2. If you have been out of school for some time, you may have to be more enterprising in obtaining appropriate letters of recommendations (see chapters 4 and 6).

January/February

_____ Begin to prepare for possible preselection interviews (see chapter 7).

_____ Contact professors whom you have asked to submit letters of recommendation. Confirm that they were sent and thank those who sent them.

_____ Follow up to confirm that your completed applications were received.

_____ Attend any preselection interviews you are invited to.

March

_____ Follow the procedures outlined in chapter 7 for accepting and declining offers.

_____ If you are not accepted at any of the schools of your choice, consider the options outlined in chapter 7.

April

_____ Finalize your financial arrangements for attending graduate school.

_____ Call or write the people who wrote your letters of recommendation and inform them of the outcome.

_____ Celebrate (or regroup).

Note. This timetable was adapted from _Preparing for Graduate Study in Psychology: Not for Seniors Only!_ (pp. 32–33) by B. R. Fretz and D. J. Stang, 1980, Washington, DC: American Psychological Association.

Appendix B: A Student's Guide to the APA Divisions

The many specialized interests of psychologists are represented through the APA's divisions. APA student affiliates are strongly encouraged to apply for affiliation in as many divisions as they wish. The APA Division Services Office provides information for and about divisions. You can reach the office by writing to Division Services, APA, 750 First Street, NE, Washington, DC 20002-4242, or by calling (202)336-6013.

Each of the following divisions has a "student affiliate" or a "general affiliate" category under which a student may apply. These divisions welcome active student involvement. Division 13, Consulting Psychology, and Division 42, Psychologists in Independent Practice, do not have student affiliates. There are no Divisions 4 and 11.

1. General Psychology

The goal of Division 1 is to unify and improve communication among the diverse specialities of psychology by stressing the underlying themes that make us all psychologists. We are concerned with "big picture" issues that cross specialty boundaries. Student affiliates are welcomed from all areas of psychology, including those who are planning careers in academic psychology, professional practice, and the public interest. Student affiliates receive the Division 1 bulletin *The General Psychologist* three times a year.

2. Teaching of Psychology

Division 2 seeks to bridge the gap between research and the teaching of psychology by encouraging research and its application to the benefit of the teaching profession. Student affiliation is open to graduate students of psychology, and includes a subscription to the journal *Teaching of Psychology*. Division 2 sponsors an annual awards program that includes an award for a graduate teaching assistant. Students sit on the division's committees and task forces.

3. Experimental Psychology

Members of Division 3 are united by a commitment to the development of experimental psychology as a science. Student affiliates of the APA can be affiliates of the division; affiliation includes a subscription to the *Division of Experimental Psychology Newsletter*.

5. Evaluation, Measurement, and Statistics

The division promotes high standards in both research and practical applications of psychological evaluation, measurement, and statistics. Graduate students in psychology or a related field are welcome to join. The division sponsors a yearly award with a cash prize of $500 for a completed dissertation on a relevant subject. The student affiliate fee includes a subscription to the newsletter *The Score*.

6. Physiological and Comparative Psychology

Any interested student may join this division. The subdisciplines of perception and learning, neuroscience, cognitive psychology, and comparative psychology are represented by the members of Division 6. Students receive the division's newsletter *The Physiological and Comparative Psychologist* and compete for the Donald O. Hebb student award.

7. Developmental Psychology

Division 7 promotes research in developmental psychology and its application to education, child care, policy, and related settings. Each year the division selects an outstanding new doctoral dissertation for its Dissertation Award. The division automatically sends a *Guide to Graduate Programs in Developmental Psychology* to new undergraduate affiliates, and to graduate affiliates upon request. Students whose work is primarily developmental in focus are invited to join the division; they receive a subscription to the *Division 7 Newsletter*, which contains substantive articles relevant to developmental psychology, as well as announcements of awards, funding and employment opportunities, conferences, and Division 7 activities.

8. The Society for Personality and Social Psychology

This division seeks to advance the progress of theory, basic and applied research, and practice in the field of personality and social psychology. Affiliation includes subscriptions to the division newsletter, *Dialogue*, and to its journal, *Personality and Social Psychology Bulletin*, and is open to all interested students. The Division sponsors an annual student publication award with a cash prize of $200.

9. Society for the Psychological Study of Social Issues

This society is concerned with the psychological aspects of important social issues. Students can join and receive all the privileges of full members, including the *SPSSI Newsletter* and the *Journal of Social Issues*.

10. Psychology and the Arts

This division seeks to advance the relationship between psychology and the arts through research and practical applications. The division offers the annual Daniel E. Berlyne Award for an outstanding dissertation by a graduate student or new PhD; winners of the Berlyne award present their papers at the APA convention. Affiliation, open to all interested students, includes a subscription to the division newsletter.

12. Clinical Psychology

Members are active in practice, research, teaching, administration, and/ or study in clinical psychology. Affiliation, open to graduate students enrolled in recognized clinical psychology programs, includes a subscription to the journal *The Clinical Psychology Review* and the newsletter *Clinical Psychology Bulletin*. Students may also choose to join one of six sections: Clinical Child; Clinical Geropsychology; Society for a Science of Clinical Psychology; Clinical Psychology of Women; Pediatric Psychology; and Racial/Ethnic and Cultural Issues.

14. Society for Industrial and Organizational Psychology

Members espouse the scientist–practitioner model in the application of psychology to all types of organizations providing goods or services, such as manufacturing concerns, commercial enterprises, labor unions or trade associations, and public agencies. Graduate or undergraduate students in related programs can join; they receive a subscription to the newsletter *The Industrial–Organizational Psychologist* and reduced registration at Division 14's spring conference. A student dissertation award is given yearly.

15. Educational Psychology

Division 15 welcomes psychologists interested in research, teaching, or practice in educational settings at all levels. Student affiliates must be in graduate programs in psychology and endorsed by a Division 15 member. Student affiliates receive the newsletter, the division journal *The Educational Psychologist*, and a free *Job Hunter's Guide*. There is a graduate dissertation award and a graduate student committee in which student affiliates may participate.

16. School Psychology

Scientific–practitioner psychologists whose major professional interests lie with children, families, and the schooling process invite students who are preparing for a career in school psychology to join. The division, in conjunction with the National Association of School Psychologists, compiles a listing of school psychology doctoral internships for the use of its student affiliates. The quarterly publications *School Psychology Quarterly* and *The School Psychologist* are sent to all members and affiliates.

17. Counseling Psychology

The division comprises psychologists who specialize in counseling to enhance education, training, scientific investigation, and practice. Twenty informal interest groups focus on a variety of specialties. Student affiliation is open to doctoral students in counseling psychology or counselor education programs; the yearly fee includes a subscription to the newsletter. A subscription to the journal is also available for a small additional charge. Student representatives provide input for a column in the newsletter and a student symposium held at the APA convention. One student sits as a nonvoting member of the division's executive board. An annual award with a cash prize of $500 is given by Consulting Psychologists Press for an independent research article by a graduate student enrolled in a counseling psychology program.

18. Psychologists in Public Service

Members work in a variety of settings responding to the needs of the public, particularly in advocating for mental health needs. Students may also elect to join any of five sections: Community and State Hospital Psychologists; Criminal Justice; Police and Public Safety; Evaluation; and VA Psychologists. The division newsletter, *Public Service Psychology*, is sent to members and affiliates.

19. Military Psychology

Military issues such as management, providing mental health services, advising senior military commands, and research on the military are some of the interests of Division 19's membership who work in military installations, with Congressional committees, and as consultants. Students may join as affiliates; they receive the division newsletter, *The Military Psychologist*, and the journal *Military Psychology*.

20. Adult Development and Aging

Members are devoted to the study of psychological development and change throughout the adult years and include psychologists who provide services to older adults, conduct research on adult development and aging, or teach life span development and aging. Student affiliates receive the quarterly *Adult Development and Aging News* and may compete for the annual student research award. The division publishes *A Guide to Doctoral Study in Adult Development and Aging*, which can be a valuable resource to undergraduates in selecting a program.

21. Applied Experimental and Engineering Psychology

The central issues of this division concern the characteristics, design, and use of environments where people work and live. Student affiliates of the APA who join Division 21 receive reduced rates at the division's annual midyear meeting in Washington, DC, the journal *PsycSCAN: Applied Experimental and Engineering Psychology*, and the *Division 21 Newsletter* and are eligible to win a $200 undergraduate student award for the best paper on applied experimental and engineering psychology and an invitation to present their paper at the APP convention.

22. Rehabilitation Psychology

Psychologists interested in the psychological aspects of disability come together to serve people with disabilities, educate the public about them, and develop high standards for their treatment. Affiliation is open to APA student affiliates and includes the division's quarterly journal, *Rehabilitation Psychology*, and the newsletter, *Rehabilitation Psychology News*. An annual "young researcher" award is given to an outstanding dissertation in the area of rehabilitation psychology.

23. Consumer Psychology

Student affiliates receive the division's two quarterly publications, *The Journal of Consumer Psychology* and the newsletter *The Communicator*. The division offers a significant discount to its members on the *Journal of Consumer Research* and *Psychology and Marketing* and also offers its newly revised brochure "Careers in Consumer Psychology."

24. Theoretical and Philosophical Psychology

This division encourages and facilitates informed exploration and discussion of psychological theories and issues in both their scientific and philosophical dimensions and interrelationships. All APA student affiliates interested in theoretical and philosophical psychology are invited to join. Students receive the division newsletter and the *Journal of Theoretical and Philosophical Psychology*. Students may also compete for a cash award for the best student paper on a related topic.

25. Experimental Analysis of Behavior

This division promotes basic research, both animal and human, in the experimental analysis of behavior; it encourages the application of the results of such research to human affairs, and cooperates with other disciplines whose interests overlap with those of the division. The division publishes *The Recorder*, a newsletter distributed three times a year to all members and affiliates. Division 25 participates in the APA annual convention, sponsoring individual speakers, symposia, and special events, such as receptions and an annual dinner. Division 25 sponsors four annual awards (B. F. Skinner New Researcher Award, Fred S. Keller Behavioral Education Award, Don Hake Basic/Applied Research Award, Analysis of Behavior Dissertation Award). Each award provides for an honorarium, a certificate of recognition, and an invitation to present an invited address at the APA convention. Student affiliation and involvement in the division are encouraged.

26. History of Psychology

The division seeks to extend the awareness and appreciation of the history of psychology as an aid to understanding contemporary psychology, psychology's relation to other scientific fields, and its role in society. Student affiliates of the division receive the *History of Psychology Newsletter*, published three to four times per year. Students are encouraged to submit papers for the APA annual convention program, and small grants are awarded to subsidize those students whose papers have been selected for presentation.

27. Society for Community Research and Action: Division of Community Psychology

The society encourages the development of theory, research, and practice relevant to the reciprocal relationships between individuals and the social system that constitutes the community; and supports the activities of 23 regional groups that promote communication among community psychologists in six U.S. regions, Canada, Western Europe, and the South Pacific. Students at the graduate level are invited to join. They receive the *American Journal of Community Psychology*, the *Community Psychologist*, and reduced rates at the division's biennial conference.

28. Psychopharmacology and Substance Abuse

The division is concerned with the teaching, research, and dissemination of information on the behavioral effects of pharmacological agents in both the laboratory and the clinic. Students who are APA affiliates may join at no cost. *The Psychopharmacology Newsletter*, which is sent to affiliates, contains listings of job openings and postdoctoral training opportunities. An annual postdoctoral award is given by the division.

29. Psychotherapy

Division 29 promotes education, research, high standards of practice, and exchange of information. All psychology students are welcome to join; the division offers a general and an ethnic minority affiliation. Students receive the *Psychotherapy Bulletin* (which features a student section) and the journal *Psychotherapy: Theory, Research & Practice*, as well as special rates for the division's midyear meeting. Division 29 sponsors an annual student paper competition, with prizes awarded to first- and second-place winners in both a general and an ethnic minority category, presented at a special student social hour at the annual APA convention.

30. Psychological Hypnosis

Division 30 is devoted to the exchange of scientific information on hypnosis, advancing appropriate teaching and research in hypnosis, and developing high standards for the practice of hypnosis. Students who are APA student affiliates are welcome to join the division at no additional cost. A graduate student award is presented annually for the best original paper on hypnosis. Division 30's quarterly newsletter, *Psychological Hypnosis*, is sent to student affiliates.

31. State Psychological Association Affairs

The division provides advocacy for state or provincial psychological associations, representing their interests within APA's governance structure, and recognizes the contributions of these associations. Students who are affiliates of their state association are welcome to join as division affiliates; they receive the newsletter *State Psychological Association Affairs*.

32. Humanistic Psychology

Division 32 welcomes all students who are eligible for APA student affiliation. Humanistic psychology recognizes the full richness of the human experience; its foundations include philosophical humanism, existentialism, and phenomenology. The division seeks to contribute to psychotherapy, education, theory/philosophy, research, organization and management, and social responsibility and change. Students receive the division's journal, *The Humanistic Psychologist*, three times per year and the division newsletter twice a year.

33. Mental Retardation and Developmental Disabilities

Division 33 seeks to advance psychology in the treatment of mental retardation and developmental disabilities. The division has five special interest groups on Behavior Modification and Technology; Dual Diagnosis; Early Intervention; Aging and Adult Development; and Transition Into Adulthood. Students with a BA in psychology or a related field can become affiliates of the division with the endorsement of a faculty member. Students receive the newsletter *Psychology in Mental Retardation and Developmental Disabilities*.

34. Population and Environmental Psychology

Environmental toxins, contextual theories and methods, environmental cognition and perception, ecological psychology, and design are some of the varied interests of the division. Students enrolled in a population psychology or environmental psychology program (or in a related field of study) are eligible for affiliation. They receive the newsletter and a discount on EDRA's journal, *Environment & Behavior*. The division awards a $100 prize for an outstanding student paper each year, which is included in the poster session at the APA convention.

35. Psychology of Women

The division develops a comprehensive approach to understanding women's psychological and social needs and issues. It has established two sections: Black Women, and Feminist Training and Practice. Students are welcome to join. *The Division 35 Newsletter* and the journal *Psychology of Women Quarterly* are included in the yearly fee. An annual cash award is given for an outstanding research paper on the psychology of women or on gender issues. The division provides a "mentoring" network in which students' interests are matched with division members willing to advise them on careers in research, academia, or practice.

36. Psychology of Religion

Members are psychologists who believe that religion is an important and interesting phenomenon in personal, social, and cultural life; some affiliates are clergy with an interest in psychology, and others are students of theology or psychology. The division is nondenominational, and anyone with an interest in these issues is invited to join. Cost for student affiliation includes a subscription to the quarterly newsletter.

37. Child, Youth, and Family Services

The division is concerned with professional and scientific issues relative to services and service structures for children and youth. It seeks to advance research, education, training, and practice and provide a vehicle for relating psychological knowledge to other fields such as anthropology, law, and pediatrics. All students of psychology are invited to join; they receive the newsletter, *Division of Child, Youth and Family Services Quarterly*. There is a yearly prize for outstanding student paper: $500 cash, a free one-year affiliation to the division, and the opportunity to present the paper at the APA convention.

38. Health Psychology

This division seeks to advance contributions of psychology to the understanding of health and illness and encourages the integration of biomedical information about health and illness with current psychological knowledge. Membership requires the signature of a faculty member on the application. An award is given at the APA convention to the best student paper on health psychology. Both the newsletter and the journal *Health Psychology* are included in the student fee. The division maintains a listing of internships available from pre- to postdoctoral.

39. Psychoanalysis

Founded in 1979, the division encompasses the diversity and richness of psychoanalytic theory, research, and clinical practive. The seven sections within Division 39 represent members' broad interests: Psychologist–Psychoanalyst Practitioners; Childhood and Adolescence; Women and Psychoanalysis; Local Chapters; Psychologist–Psychoanalysts Forum; Psychoanalytic Research Society; Psychoanalysis and Groups. There are over 3,700 members of Division 39 and 27 local chapters throughout the United States. A four-day Spring Meeting is held annually. Student members receive a discounted fee for the Spring Meeting, and the journals *Psychoanalytic Psychology* and *Psychoanalytic Abstracts*, as well as the newsletter *Psychologist–Psychoanalyst*. Students do not have to be affiliates of the APA to join Division 39.

40. Clinical Neuropsychology

This division advances the contributions of psychology to the understanding of neurologically related behavior disorders through research, education, and services. The division publishes a semiannual newsletter, *Division of Clinical Neuropsychology* (which has a listing of postdoctoral programs having a neurological orientation). Student affiliates of the APA may join the division at no cost but, because of budget limitations, may not always receive the newsletter. An annual $100 student award is given to the best student paper on clinical neuropsychology presented at the APA convention.

41. American Psychology–Law Society

Students in psychology, law, criminal justice, or sociology may become members of Division 41, which promotes the contributions of psychology to an understanding of law and legal institutions. The cost for students covers a subscription to the division newsletter and the journal *Law and Human Behavior*, a discounted registration fee for the division's biennial meeting, and eligibility for an annual award ($300 for first prize, $150 for second) for outstanding dissertations. Division 41 has a small grants-in-aid program for research in psychology and the law and provides some financial assistance to students for participation in the APA convention.

43. Family Psychology

Research, education, and service activities to individuals, couples, and families are the main interests of Division 43 members. Such areas as divorce; drug and alcohol abuse; child, spouse, and elder abuse; government policy on families; and geriatric psychology are addressed. Students of psychology who present a confirming letter of their status as students may join the division. Student affiliates receive the newsletter *Family Psychologist*. Division 43 gives an annual student research award.

44. Society for the Psychological Study of Lesbian and Gay Issues

The division is currently involved in such issues as training and guidelines in professional psychology relative to treatment of lesbians, gay men, and bisexuals; racial and ethnic minority issues; research guidelines and ethical issues in research on and treatment of homosexuals; and the impact of AIDS and its psychological implications. The division has developed the Malyon-Smith award for student research on gay and lesbian issues. The division also provides a support system for gay, lesbian, and bisexual students and participates in antidiscriminatory activism. Student affiliates receive the *SPSLGI Newsletter* three times per year.

45. Society for the Psychological Study of Ethnic Minority Issues

This division encourages contributions in psychological research as it relates to ethnic minority issues, and promotes the education and training of psychologists in areas of importance to ethnic minority populations. The division is currently active in the areas of AIDS and legislative policy on ethnic minority groups. Any psychology student with an interest in such issues can join. Students receive the division newsletter *Focus*.

46. Media Psychology

Division 46 provides a network of practitioners and scientists who are involved in communicating their ideas via the electronic, print, and broadcast media—both popular and professional. They also study the impact of media on behavior and the use of media in information dissemination. The division offers workshops for those interested in appearing in media as hosts, guest experts, reporters, columnists, and commentators. Both undergraduate and graduate students may join Division 46. Cost of affiliation includes a subscription to the newsletter *The Amplifier*.

47. Exercise and Sport Psychology

Both psychologists and exercise and sport scientists form the membership of this division, which is interested in research, teaching, and service in this area. The division has committees on ethnic minorities, gender issues, education and training, and physically disabled sport participants. The APA Running Psychologists are an affiliated group of Division 47. An outstanding dissertation award is given yearly on the topic of sport or exercise psychology.

48. Peace Psychology

The division encourages research, education, and training on issues concerning peace; nonviolent conflict resolution; reconciliation; and the causes, consequences, and prevention of war and other forms of destructive conflict. Students, who are encouraged to participate in the activities of this division, receive the division's newsletter.

49. Group Psychology and Group Psychotherapy

The division provides a forum for psychologists interested in research, teaching, and practice in group psychology and group psychotherapy.

Division 49's leadership is currently at work developing initial publications, committees, and special projects. Students are encouraged to join division committees and assist in building the framework of the division.

50. Psychology of Addictive Behaviors

This division promotes advances in research, professional training, and clinical practice within the broad range of addictive behaviors including problematic use of alcohol, nicotine, and other drugs; or disorders involving gambling, eating, sexual behavior, or spending. Currently enrolled students in psychology are eligible for student affiliate membership status. Membership includes a subscription to the quarterly peer-reviewed journal *Psychology of Addictive Behaviors* and the semiannual newsletter of the division.

Appendix C: State and Provincial Boards and Agencies for the Statutory Licensure or Certification of Psychologists

ALABAMA
Board of Examiners in Psychology
401 Interstate Park Drive
Montgomery, AL 36109
(205) 242-4127

ALASKA
Department of Commerce and
  Economic Development
Division of Occupational Licensing
Board of Psychologists and
  Psychological Associate Examiners
P.O. Box 110806
Juneau, AK 99811-0806
(907) 465-2551

ARIZONA
Board of Psychologist Examiners
1645 West Jefferson, Room 410
Phoenix, AZ 85007
(602) 542-3095

ARKANSAS
Department of Professional
  Regulation
Board of Examiners in Psychology
101 E. Capitol Ave., Suite 415
Little Rock, AR 72201-3823
(501) 682-6167

CALIFORNIA
Board of Psychology
1426 Howe Avenue, Suite 54
Sacramento, CA 95825-3236
(916) 263-2699

COLORADO
Board of Psychologists Examiners
1560 Broadway, Suite 1340
Denver, CO 80202
(303) 894-7766

CONNECTICUT
Department of Health Services
Connecticut Psychology Licensure
150 Washington Street
Hartford, CT 06106
(203) 566-1039

DELAWARE
Board of Examiners of Psychologists
Margaret O'Neil Building
P.O. Box 1401
Dover, DE 19903
(302) 739-4796

DISTRICT OF COLUMBIA
Board of Psychological Examiners
614 H Street, NW, Room 910
Washington, DC 20001
(202) 727-7823/24

FLORIDA
Board of Psychological Examiners
Department of Professional
  Regulation
1940 North Monroe Street
Tallahassee, FL 32399-0788
(904) 922-6728

GEORGIA
Board of Examiners of Psychologists
State Examining Board
166 Pryor Street, SW
Atlanta, GA 30303
(404) 656-3933

HAWAII
Department of Commerce and
  Consumer Affairs
Board of Psychology
P.O. Box 3469
Honolulu, HI 96801
(808) 586-2702

IDAHO
Bureau of Occupational Licenses
Board of Psychologist Examiners
2417 Bank Drive, Room 312
Boise, ID 83705
(208) 334-3233

ILLINOIS
Clinical Psychologists Licensing and
  Disciplinary Committee
Department of Professional
  Regulation
320 W. Washington St., 3rd Floor
Springfield, IL 62786
(217) 785-0872

INDIANA
State Psychology Board
402 W. Washington St., #401
Indianapolis, IN 46204
(317) 232-2960

IOWA
Board of Psychology Examiners
Professional Licensure
Department of Public Health
Lucas State Office Building
Des Moines, IA 50319-0075
(515) 281-4401

KANSAS
Behavioral Science Regulatory Board
900 Jackson, Room 855-S
Topeka, KS 66612
(913) 296-3240

KENTUCKY
State Board of Psychology
P.O. Box 456
Frankfort, KY 40602-0456
(502) 564-3296

LOUISIANA
Board of Examiners of Psychologists
11853 Bricksome Ave., Suite B
Baton Rouge, LA 70816
(504) 293-2238

MAINE
Department of Business,
  Occupational and Professional
  Regulation
State House Station #35
Augusta, ME 04333
(207) 582-8723

MARYLAND
Board of Examiners of Psychologists
4201 Patterson Avenue
Baltimore, MD 21215-2299
(410) 764-4787

MASSACHUSETTS
Board of Registration of Psychologists
100 Cambridge St., 15th Floor
Boston, MA 02202
(617) 727-9925

MICHIGAN
Board of Psychology
Department of Licensing and
  Regulation
P.O. Box 30018
Lansing, MI 48909
(517) 373-3596

MINNESOTA
Board of Psychology
2700 University Ave., W., Room 101
St. Paul, MN 55114
(612) 642-0587

MISSISSIPPI
Board of Psychological Examiners
812 North President Street
Jackson, MS 39202
(601) 353-8871

MISSOURI
State Committee of Psychologists
P.O. Box 153
Jefferson City, MO 65102
(314) 751-0099

MONTANA
Board of Psychologists
Arcade Building—Lower Level
111 N. Last Chance Gulch
Helena, MT 59620-0407
(406) 444-5436

NEBRASKA
Board of Examining Psychologists
Bureau of Examining Board
301 Centennial Mall South
P.O. Box 95007
Lincoln, NE 68509-5007
(402) 471-2115

NEVADA
Board of Psychological Examiners
798 Sutro, Suite I
Reno, NV 89512
(702) 688-1268

NEW HAMPSHIRE
Board of Examiners of Psychology
Box 457
105 Pleasant Street
Concord, NH 03301
(603) 226-2599

NEW JERSEY
Board of Psychological Examiners
P.O. Box 45017
Newark, NJ 07101
(201) 504-6470

NEW MEXICO
Board of Psychologists Examiners
P.O. Box 25101
Santa Fe, NM 87504
(505) 827-7163

NEW YORK
Board for Psychology
Cultural Education Center, Rm. 3041
Albany, NY 12230
(518) 474-3866

NORTH CAROLINA
State Board of Examiners of
    Practicing Psychologists
University Hall
Appalachian State University
Boone, NC 28608
(704) 262-2258

NORTH DAKOTA
Board of Psychologist Examiners
1406 Second Street, NW
Mandan, ND 58554
(701) 663-2321 Ext. 202

OHIO
State Board of Psychology
77 South High Street, 18th Fl.
Columbus, OH 43266-0321
(614) 466-8808

OKLAHOMA
Board of Examiners of Psychologists
P.O. Box 53551
Oklahoma City, OK 73152
(405) 271-6118

OREGON
Board of Psychologist Examiners
895 Summer Street, NE
Salem, OR 97310
(503) 378-4154

PENNSYLVANIA
State Board of Psychology
P.O. Box 2649
Harrisburg, PA 17105-2649
(717) 783-7155

RHODE ISLAND
Board of Psychology
Division of Professional Regulation
Cannon Building, Room 104
3 Capitol Hill
Providence, RI 02908-5097
(401) 277-2827

SOUTH CAROLINA
Board of Examiners in Psychology
P.O. Box 11477
Columbia, SC 29211
(803) 253-6313

SOUTH DAKOTA
Board of Examiners of Psychologists
P.O. Box 654
Spearfish, SD 57783-0654
(605) 642-1600

TENNESSEE
Board of Examiners in Psychology
283 Plus Park Blvd.
Nashville, TN 37219-5407
(615) 367-6291

TEXAS
Board of Examiners of Psychologists
9101 Burnet Road, Suite 212
Austin, TX 78758
(512) 835-2036

UTAH
Psychology Examining Committee
Division of Occupational and
   Professional Licensing
160 East, 300 South
P.O. Box 45802
Salt Lake City, UT 84145
(801) 530-6628

VERMONT
Board of Psychologist Examiners
Licensing and Registration Division
Office of the Secretary of State
26 Terrace Street
Pavilion Office Building
Montpelier, VT 05602
(802) 828-2373

VIRGINIA
Board of Psychology
1601 Rolling Hills Dr., Suite 200
Richmond, VA 23229-5005
(804) 662-9913

WASHINGTON
Examining Board of Psychology
Professional Licensing Division
1300 Quince Street, SE
Olympia, WA 98504-7868
(206) 753-3095

WEST VIRGINIA
Board of Examiners of Psychologists
709 Pike Street
Barrackwille, WV 26559
(304) 367-2709

WISCONSIN
Psychology Examining Board
P.O. Box 8935
Madison, WI 53708-8935
(608) 266-0070

WYOMING
Board of Psychologist Examiners
Barrett Building
2301 Central Avenue
Cheyenne, WY 82002
(307) 777-6529

Canadian Provinces/Territories

ALBERTA
Professional Examination Office
Suite 740
8303-112 Street
Edmonton, Alberta T6G 1KY
(403) 429-9975

BRITISH COLUMBIA
College of Psychologists of British
   Columbia
865 West 10th Avenue, Suite 10
Vancouver, BC V5Z 1L7
(604) 877-1454

MANITOBA
Psychological Association of Manitoba
1800-155 Carlton Street
Winnipeg, Manitoba R3C 3H8
(204) 947-3698

NEW BRUNSWICK
College of Psychologists of New
   Brunswick
P.O. Box 1194, Station A
Fredericton, New Brunswick
E3B 1B0
(506) 459-1994

NOVA SCOTIA
Nova Scotia Board of Examiners in
  Psychology
Box 27124
Halifax, Nova Scotia B3H 4M8
(902) 423-2238

NORTHWEST TERRITORIES
Registrar of Psychologists
Department of Safety and Public
  Services
Government of Northwest Territories
Yellowknife, Northwest Territories
  X1A 2L9
(403) 920-8058

ONTARIO
Board of Examiners in Psychology
1246 Yonge Street, Suite 201
Toronto, Ontario M4T 1W5
(416) 961-8817

QUEBEC
Corporation Professionnelle des
  Psychologues du Québec
1100, rue Beaumont, Bureau 510
Ville Mont-Royal, Québec H3P 3E5
(514) 738-1881

SASKATCHEWAN
Saskatchewan Psychological
  Association
Mental Health Centre
P.O. Box 1056
Weyburn, Saskatchewan S4H 2L4
(306) 842-5461

Appendix D: Sample Recommendation Form

Applicant's name _____

Name of person completing this form _____

SAMPLE RECOMMENDATION FORM

To the applicant: This form should be given to professors who are able to comment on your qualifications for graduate study in psychology. You should not request a recommendation from a nonacademic person unless you have been away from an academic institution for some time. For the convenience of the person completing this form, you should include a stamped envelope addressed to each graduate program to which you are applying.

Under the federal Family Educational Rights and Privacy Act of 1974, students are entitled to review their records, including letters of recommendation. However, those writing recommendations and those assessing recommendations may attach more significance to them if it is known that the recommendations will remain confidential. It is your option to waive your right to access to these recommendations or to decline to do so. Please mark the appropriate phrase below, indicating your choice of option, and sign your name:

☐ I waive my right to review of this recommendation.
☐ I do *not* waive my right to review of this recommendation.

Date _____ Applicant's Signature _____

Name (print) _____

Intended field of study: _____

Degree sought (check one): Master's ☐   Doctorate ☐

Date by which this form should reach the applicant's graduate schools: _____

Application for:

Admission and Fellowship ☐   Admission only ☐   Fellowship only ☐

RECOMMENDATION

1. I have known the applicant for _____ years, _____ months.
2. I know the applicant: slightly ☐   fairly well ☐   very well ☐

continued

Applicant's name _____

Name of person completing this form _____

3. I have known the applicant:
   - ☐ As an undergraduate student. ☐ As a teaching assistant.
   - ☐ As a graduate student. ☐ As an advisee.
   - ☐ Other _____
4. The applicant has taken:
   none of my classes ☐   one of my classes ☐   two or more of my classes ☐
5. Indicate the population with which the applicant is being compared in this rating:
   - ☐ Undergraduate students whom I have taught or known.
   - ☐ Graduate students whom I have taught or known.
   - ☐ All students, graduate and undergraduate, whom I have taught or known.
   - ☐ Colleagues whom I have worked with.
6. *Critical Incidents:* For each of the following incidents, check those that you *know* from your own, direct personal experience and observation apply to this applicant.

Technical Skills

- ☐ Is skilled in the use of videotape equipment.
- ☐ Has built a piece of laboratory equipment.
- ☐ Can make electrical or plumbing repairs in the laboratory.
- ☐ Has analytical chemistry, physiological, or histological skills.
- ☐ Can use blueprints, line drawings, or schematic diagrams to build laboratory equipment.
- ☐ Uses power tools with proficiency.

Investigative Skills

- ☐ Won a prize in a science fair or contest.
- ☐ Wrote the results of a study clearly and concisely.
- ☐ Was a paid research assistant.
- ☐ Used a programmable calculator to perform a statistical test.
- ☐ Wrote a computer program in FORTRAN, COBOL, BASIC, or other *programming language.*
- ☐ Used SPSS, BMD, Miami Statistical Package, or other canned statistical packages in performing a project.

Originality

- ☐ Generates creative ideas in class discussions.
- ☐ Has devised a surgical technique, designed laboratory equipment, or developed an unusual research strategy.
- ☐ Has completed an innovative research project.
- ☐ Has won a prize for creative writing or worked on the school or local newspaper as a writer.
- ☐ Has created an original work of art or music.
- ☐ Recasts old problems in original ways.
- ☐ Other _____

continued

Applicant's name _____

Name of person completing this form _____

Social Skills

☐ Seems to be good at helping people who are upset or troubled.
☐ Is sought by students or faculty for advice.
☐ Makes and keeps friends easily.
☐ Participated in voluntary community or social service activities.
☐ Was employed as a case aide, psychiatric technician, or student assistant in a telephone hotline center, crisis counseling center, or mental health center.

Leadership and Persuasive Skills

☐ Is convincing in discussions or debate.
☐ Leads group discussions easily.
☐ Was elected an officer of an organization or to a political office.
☐ Volunteers to give oral reports.
☐ Organized a student group project.
☐ Has participated in a business venture or political campaign.

Orderliness and Clerical Skills

☐ Always completes class assignments or papers on time.
☐ Schedules own work and follows through with the schedule.
☐ Submits work that has been carefully proofread and checked for spelling or computational errors.
☐ Submits neatly prepared written reports.

Independence

☐ Tries to solve problems independently before seeking advice.
☐ Performed research with a faculty member that was not for course credit.
☐ Completed an independent project with little faculty direction.
☐ Organized a special course of readings or experiences for self.
☐ Has worked to pay tuition and expenses.
☐ Requires little direction from faculty.

Commitment to Psychology

☐ Attended a regional psychology convention as an undergraduate.
☐ Attends psychology department colloquiums.
☐ Seeks out psychological literature beyond coursework requirements.
☐ Is interested in a career of applying psychology.
☐ Is interested in a career of research in psychology.
☐ Is interested in a career of teaching psychology.

7. *Global Ratings:* Compared to the population indicated in item 5, rate this applicant on each characteristic.

CHARACTERISTIC:	Lower 50%	Upper 50%	Upper 25%	Upper 10%	Upper 5%	No Basis for Judgment
Academic Ability						
General Knowledge						

continued

Applicant's name _____

Name of person completing this form _____

Global Ratings (continued)

CHARACTERISTIC:	Lower 50%	Upper 50%	Upper 25%	Upper 10%	Upper 5%	No Basis for Judgment
Scientific Skepticism						
Oral Expression Skills						
Written Expression Skills						
Originality						
Social Awareness and Concern						
Emotional Maturity						
Desire to Achieve						
Ability to Work with Others						
Leadership Skills						
Persuasive Ability						
Independence and Initiative						
Professional Commitment						
Research Skills						
Teaching Skills						
Potential for Success						
Carefulness in Work						

8. Is the applicant's academic potential greater or less than that indicated by his/her grades? Insert an X where appropriate on the scale below.

| much less | somewhat less | equal | somewhat greater | much greater | | no basis for judgment |

9. If the applicant has had teaching experience, how would you rate his/her potential for college teaching?

Poor ☐   Fair ☐   Good ☐   Excellent ☐   Cannot determine ☐

10. If the applicant has had research experience, how would you rate his/her research potential?

Poor ☐   Fair ☐   Good ☐   Excellent ☐   Cannot determine ☐

11. How would you rate the applicant's potential for work in applied research settings?

Poor ☐   Fair ☐   Good ☐   Excellent ☐   Cannot determine ☐

continued

Applicant's name _____

Name of person completing this form _____

12. How would you rate the applicant's potential for clinical or counseling work?
Poor ☐   Fair ☐   Good ☐   Excellent ☐   Cannot determine ☐

13. Indicate the strength of your overall endorsement of the applicant.
☐ Not recommended
☐ Recommended with some reservations
☐ Recommended
☐ Highly recommended

14. The space below is supplied for any additional information you may wish to provide, such as explanations of any of the critical incidents checked. The most important information you can provide about this applicant is information that is not reflected in the applicant's transcript and test scores (i.e., work done outside of class and other characteristics you believe are related to success in graduate school). Attach additional pages if necessary.

_____

_____

_____

_____

_____

_____

_____

_____

_____

_____

_____

_____

_____

Signature of person completing this form _____ Title _____

Name (print) _____

Institution or affiliation _____

Please check to make sure items are completed correctly and return this form to the graduate schools for which the applicant has supplied stamped, addressed envelopes.

Thank you for completing this form.

Note. This form was adapted from *Preparing for Graduate Study in Psychology: Not for Seniors Only!* (pp. 49–54) by B. R. Fretz and D. J. Stang, 1980, Washington, DC: American Psychological Association.

Appendix E: The Minority Fellowship Program

The Minority Fellowship Program (MFP) was founded in 1974 and is jointly funded by the National Institute of Mental Health (NIMH) and the American Psychological Association (APA). The program was established to improve and enlarge educational opportunities for members of ethnic minority groups who wish to study psychology and neuroscience. As of 1993, the MFP has provided financial support to over 758 Fellows. Of this group, 56% have obtained their doctorate and an additional 40% are still in training. Annually, the program receives over 500 applications and makes approximately 45 new awards. Students eligible for fellowships are American citizens and residents holding permanent visas; they include, but are not limited to, those who are Black, Hispanic, American Indian, Alaskan Native, Asian American, and Pacific Islander.

The program offers support to individuals who are receiving training in three different areas of study: clinical and research training in psychology and research training in neuroscience. New psychology students must gain admission to a graduate program and express a commitment to research, delivery of clinical services, and involvement in minority issues in mental health and behavioral sciences. Neuroscience students must gain admission to a graduate program and express a commitment to neuroscience research. Students in clinical training must be enrolled in a training program that is accredited by the APA. Students in neuroscience training should select a program that is listed in the handbook *Neuroscience Training Programs in North America* (see Resources).

Trainees receive up to three years of support (up to $8,800 for a 12-month student) and can also receive funding for and assistance with a number of other enrichment activities. These include travel expenses to the APA convention or to regional meetings to present papers, and funding to complete dissertation research. Clinical students preparing for their internship are assisted in locating a suitable site. All clinical and research psychology students are eligible for funding support for their dissertation research. Current trainees are afforded opportunities to participate in professional association meetings. Others, such as the neuroscience trainees, participate in summer research.

Following the receipt of their doctorate degrees, trainees are required to perform payback service as mandated by the NIMH, the federal funding source that supports their training. This allows trainees to be involved in professional career paths and to use their training to serve ethnic minority communities. Clinical trainees must provide one year of service for each year of support they receive from the MFP. The clinical payback can be fulfilled by either by providing direct service to an underserved population or by teaching or conducting research. The research trainees do not have to provide payback service for their first year of support, and they are allowed to either teach or conduct research as a means of completing the payback for the second and third years of funding they received.

For applications and further information, write to the Minority Fellowship Program, American Psychological Association, 750 First Street, NE, Washington, DC 20002-4242, or call (202) 336-6027.

Index